FROM FATHER TO SON

17 Lessons for Successful Living

Dr Jaimie Oliver Garande

authorHOUSE®

AuthorHouse™ UK Ltd.
500 Avebury Boulevard
Central Milton Keynes, MK9 2BE
www.authorhouse.co.uk
Phone: 08001974150

First published by AuthorHouse 8/13/2009

ISBN: 978-1-4389-8838-2 (sc)

This book is printed on acid-free paper.

Table of Contents

Preface

*"I talk and talk and talk, and I haven't taught people in 50 years what
my father taught by example in one week."* **Mario Cuomo**

*"My son, forget not my law but let your heart keep my commandments: For length
of days and long life and peace shall they add to thee."* (Proverbs 3:1-2)

I can say with absolute certainty that there is no human relationship that will more dramatically affect a man's life than the relationship he has or does not have with his father. Indeed there is not much else that can be said about absentee fathers that has not already been said so many times before. Their absence has a devastating impact on those they leave behind. By common consent it is far and away the most significant social problem facing our society today. Children who live away from their fathers are more likely to be poor, to experience serious educational, health, emotional and psychological problems, and to engage in criminal behaviour, than their peers who live with their fathers in a traditional family environment.

But that's not the full picture. What is also a serious cause for concern are the fathers who live in the same houses as their children but have little or no interaction with them on a day-to-day basis. Recent studies have shown that on average, a father will spend about twenty three seconds a day talking to his children. Those same children are likely to spend six hours a day watching television, getting their life lessons from a wide host of substitute 'dads'. What this clearly shows is that the father who is not actively involved in his children's lives is just as bad as the absentee father who has, for whatever reason, made the decision not to be in their lives at all.

And then obviously there are situations where a boy is deprived of his father through other events such as an untimely death. And so through nobody's fault he grows up without the male direction and guidance that every young man so desperately needs.

Whatever the cause of the fathers absence, the end result is often the same. A young man is suddenly tasked with the overwhelming responsibility of living his life successfully without having ever been adequately equipped to do so. Nature abhors a vacuum, and so inevitably there are those who will gladly step in and play the role of father to the young man, some with positive results, others less so. And as the boy grows up, he soon finds himself responsible not just for his own welfare, but possibly for that of his siblings also, and with time for his own wife and children. Now everyone looks to him for leadership and guidance. After all he is a man. But sadly he has never been shown how to make his own life work in the first place.

And so generation after generation, this depressing drama is played out, as ill-equipped men are handed the responsibility for leading their families, their communities, and sometimes even their nations, without a clear sense of how they are supposed to do so. Even within the church setting, half baked leaders, some of them well intentioned but under no spiritual authority and accountable to no one, are unleashing themselves on innocent folk in their congregations, causing untold damage, most of which goes unreported, and which is often never repaired.

Yes, the tragedy of our generation truly is fatherlessness in all its forms. I can fully understand the frustrations of the man who puts on an 'I've got it all together' front in public, and yet weeps bitter tears of frustration in private because he doesn't know how to make his life work. I empathise with the man who looks bewildered in the face of all his responsibility, and within is asking the one question every man asks himself at some stage in his life, 'but whose responsibility am I?

The way God designed the system, a man's father was tasked with providing much of the direction and wisdom that would prepare his son for adult life. He would teach him how to handle his money, how to seek his life companion and how to raise his children. By observing his father's example a son would develop the necessary character to live successfully himself. And when the time came, he would in turn pass on the wisdom he had acquired to his own children. Indeed God's endorsement of Abraham as the father of many nations and the keeper of His covenant was based on His unerring conviction that Abraham would effectively instruct his children and household in how to keep the ways of the Lord.

But as we all know, the reality has turned out very differently. Marriages break up and children often end up in separate homes from their fathers. Children are conceived out of wedlock and the fathers refuse to take responsibility for their offspring. Sickness, death and incarceration are all other factors that render many fathers incapable of fulfilling their roles. The end result is that we now have millions of men who have never been truly fathered.

Becoming a man is about more than just the ability to sire children. That's the easy part. Manhood will invariably require empowerment with specific tools that will then put you on the road to true success. Teachers, extended family members, and friends all have their part to play in this equipping process. But unlike previous cultural regimes that had a structured apprentice style approach to teaching life lessons, much of the preparation young men get today is haphazard and often leaves its pupils more confused than before.

I have had the opportunity to work in various capacities with many young boys who were from broken homes and subsequently became wards of the state, moving repeatedly from one confusing environment to another. I have witnessed first hand the abject despair, uncertainty and hopelessness that is their daily reality. Very few escape the lure of a life on the outskirts of mainstream society and many others bear the scars of their experiences for the rest of their lives. There are a few success stories, but they are few and far between. I am not embellishing when I say that in eight out of ten of these cases, the root cause of the instability they endured was that there was no strong male figure present to guide these young boys in their formative years.

And therein lies the great conundrum. The wonderful beauty and innocence of youth scarred by the unfortunate reality that so many of them will have that innocence stripped away by having to grow up too soon, unwanted and unnurtured, no better prepared for life than their fathers were, and just as likely to make exactly the same mistakes their fathers made.

And so an idea was conceived in my mind. Might there be need for some kind of resource that would act as a guide to provide answers to some of the more common questions that fathers would naturally be expected to answer? It would give young men pointers for their lives that would assist them on their journey to success and significance. It would help them to unravel the intricacies of issues ranging from marriage to money, religion to relationships. I talked to men of all ages, soliciting their opinions on whether they thought this might be of any use. The answer was a resounding yes. But what surprised me more than anything else was that although I had assumed that it was young men who would be keen on the idea and need such a resource more, I soon realised that men much older were asking the same questions. It's not just boys who need a father's guidance. Men do too.

Consequently I have written this book for men of all ages. Whether you are fourteen or forty this book is for you. I address you all as men, because if you aren't a man today, someday you will be. And every one of you will find something in here that speaks more strongly to you than everything else I have written. Take that lesson to heart.

Now more than ever I believe that if men can be appropriately empowered and educated, they can play a significant part in providing much needed answers to their women and children. Much of the wisdom contained in here is taken unashamedly and unapologetically from the Bible. I can think of no one who is better qualified to give us wisdom on how to become real men than the One who created us and who holds the wisdom of the ages in His awesome hands.

Also included are many other stories and anecdotes that have inspired me over the years, and that I am sure will inspire you too. Let's face it, we all love a great story. They have a way of bringing truths home where other mediums often fail. Eric Hoffer put it like this:

> *"Man is eminently a storyteller. His search for a purpose, a cause, an ideal, a mission and the like is largely a search for a plot and a pattern in the development of his life story".* (**The Passionate State of the Mind**)

This book was never designed to answer all the questions that a man would have. No resource can claim to do that. No book can replace the role of a flesh and blood father who would instruct his son, discipline him, inspire him and love him. Even the Bible cannot replace God in our lives. True, it contains His much needed wisdom and counsel. But we still need a hands-on Daddy who will pick us up when we fall short and celebrate with us when we succeed. Maybe that's what's wrong with the many that try and implement the excellent principles given by the God of the Bible without ever getting to know the Author personally.

Neither is this work intended to be a substitute for the journey of self-discovery that every man has to go through to discover his own individual purpose. Life was never designed to be taught in its entirety - it has to be lived. What it is designed to do however, is provide a tool that will form a foundation that can be successfully built on by each man who reads it, a catalyst if you like, to guide one on the long road to living a victorious life. If one man reads this and is inspired to make his life work, then the hundreds of hours spent in research, prayer and private reflection would have all been worth it.

It would be remiss of me not to mention and applaud the millions of men around the world who have taken up the mantle of responsibility for their sons, and are leading them on their individual journeys of self discovery and significance. Or the mothers, the grandmothers and others who for generations have stepped in and sometimes single-handedly moulded the characters of some of the most honourable men the world has been privileged to know. Men who know how to treat their wives, honour those in authority and love their children. Men who know how to make life work. I salute you all.

Jaimie Oliver Garande

Dedication

To my Dad, Joey John, an honourable man of God who never shirked his responsibilities, but hung in there during all the hard times.

Acknowledgements

It is often said that no man is an island, and nowhere is the veracity of that statement borne out more than in the publication of a book. The persons listed below have unselfishly given of their time and skills and as a result the end product is a finer piece of work than when I had sole responsibility for it.

I am indebted to my wife Nyarai for her encouragement in convincing me that I had something to offer my generation, and egging me on at every stage of the production of this work to complete it.

To my son Panashe and my daughters Tawana Frances-Jordan and Adalia-Rose who have provided the motivation for me to want to be a better father and allowed me to take time away from them to work on this book.

To my mother Frances Louise Garande for teaching me the fundamentals of proper grammar and speech and not allowing me to get away with coarse or improper language. I can still hear your corrections ringing in my head.

To my father and mother in the Lord, Dr Ramson and Pastor Linda Mumba for speaking to the giant within me and equipping me with the awareness that it is possible to live on purpose for God and do so excellently.

Finally, to all my teachers, both dead and alive who have imparted their wisdom and wit into my life.

Foreword

I know without a shadow of a doubt that you are holding in your hands one of the most significant books of our generation, a book destined to not only impact the lives of individuals but also of families, communities and nations.

Within these pages lie seeds of age-old wisdom that will speak to and empower men of every age, race and creed. With great sensitivity, skill and wisdom, Jaimie Oliver Garande demonstrates a keen understanding of the male psyche and answers such enduring questions as: What does it take to gain respect as a man? How does a man manage his responsibilities without compromising his character? How can he rise above societal pressures and expectations to become the leader he was born to be? How does a man transfer his wisdom to the next generation?

This book was written by a man who leads by example and practices what he preaches. The author's life is a testament of the veracity of the principles which he shares with the reader.

I have known Jaimie for over ten years. During our first encounter in London, I was immediately struck by his engaging personality and his heart for people. Jaimie is not only a concerned onlooker, but a man who cares enough to reach out and empower others. He is a mentor at heart.

Over the years, I have grown to respect him as a man of integrity, humility and great wisdom. As a visionary, he not only concerns himself with the issues of his society, but also of the affairs of the generations to come.

Through this book, he leads a rally call for men to build a lasting legacy.

From Father to Son is a generous act to impart wisdom and thereby positively affect society, one person at a time. Be inspired!

Neverl Kambasha

Founder of Beryl Capital Finance and Rehoboth Ministries

Johannesburg, South Africa

04 March 2009

Lesson 1 – A man and his philosophy

'For as he thinks in his heart, so is he.' **(Proverbs 23:7)**

F.W. Woolworth began as a clerk in a hardware store. The annual inventory showed that the store was stocked with thousands of dollars of merchandise that was out of date and practically useless. "'Lets run a bargain sale," he suggested to the owner "and sell off all of this old merchandise." The owner rejected the idea, but Woolworth was persistent. He kept after the store owner until it was agreed that the plan could be tried out with a few of the very oldest items.

A long table was built down the middle of the store and every item on it was priced at ten cents. The goods went so fast that Woolworth got permission to run a second sale, which also went over with a bang. Then he proposed to the owner that they go into partnership with a five and ten cent store, with Woolworth supplying the management and the store owner supplying the capital. "No!" shouted the owner. "The plan will never work, because you can't find enough items to sell at a nickel and a dime".

Woolworth went ahead by himself and piled up a fortune and started the great chain of stores that bear his name. In speaking of the transactions years later, Woolworth's old boss said woefully, "As near as I can figure it, every word I used in turning Woolworth down has cost me about a million dollars". **(Quoted from Napoleon Hill's Unlimited Success)**

A very good friend of mine, Dominic, told me about an incident that happened to him when he was growing up. His dad was a hugely successful property developer in an age when the height of most people's ambition was simply to have a roof over their heads. When he died he owned real estate worth millions of dollars. He was a huge man, nearly two metres tall and weighed about three hundred pounds. He was also an intense man, and not a little eccentric, with mesmerising

1

brown eyes that seemed to pierce right through you. When he stared at you, you felt like confessing all your sins there and then.

And yet he was a doting father and husband. His wife stood at just over five feet tall, and he worshipped the very ground that she walked on, and catered to her every need. When he went away on business trips, which was often, he would always make sure he brought his family back many exciting presents. And upon his return, they would sit up late into the night with him, and he would regale them with stories of distant lands he had visited and the amazing people he had met.

One evening, when my friend was eleven years old, his dad called him into his study, and sat him down in his favourite armchair. Surrounded by rows and rows of books, he sat down opposite his son, staring at him, not saying anything, just staring, for what seemed like an absolute eternity. Well, by this time my pal was squirming in his seat, trying to figure out what he had done wrong, and coming up with all sorts of excuses for whatever it was. Suddenly out of the blue, which rather startled him, he asked, "What do you think about most of the time?" Well, Dominic had no idea what to say. It seemed like a pretty odd question to ask especially of an eleven year old boy. What did he think about most of the time? Well, there was Ellen Daniels, the cute girl in his class that had every boy swooning over her.....

But somehow even then he knew that wasn't what his dad was talking about. So he waited expectantly. His dad was never one for protracted lectures. He got right into it.

"Son, the most important thing in any man's life is his philosophy – how he thinks. Your life will be made up of what you think about most of the time and your thoughts will determine who you become. If you remember nothing else I tell you, remember this". His dad stood up. The lesson was over. He turned to the bookshelf behind him, picked up a book, and tenderly leafed through its pages. He was soon lost in it. Dom slipped out of the study and returned to his room. But he never forgot that day, and over the years I too came to fully understand the true significance of what his dad had been trying to teach him.

This is the lesson. You will never make any lasting changes in your life until you change the way you think. All great and enduring change has to begin in the mind. John the Baptist, in heralding the coming of the Messiah admonished the Israelites to repent.

> *'In those days there appeared John the Baptist, preaching in the wilderness (desert) of Judea, and saying, "Repent (think differently, change your mind, regretting your sins and changing your conduct) for the kingdom of heaven is at hand."' (Matthew 3:1)*

John was saying that they needed to change the way they thought before they could change the way they behaved, because true repentance involves a change of mindset first. And as Jesus Himself began His ministry, He preached the same message:

> *'From that time Jesus began to preach, crying out, "Repent (change your mind for the better, heartily amend your ways, with abhorrence of your past sins) for the kingdom of heaven is at hand."' (Matthew 4:17)*

A big part of Jesus' purpose in coming to the earth was to show the world a side of His Father they had never seen before. They had always viewed God as religion had painted Him, a harsh disciplinarian with a big stick. To ever be able to see Him as a loving daddy, they would have to change the way they thought about Him.

Trying to get a person to do anything without renewing their mind on that particular issue really is an exercise in futility. For example, everyone holds stereotypes about people who are different from them. Have you bought into the idea that all black people are lazy and on welfare, or that all white people are racist and superior in their attitude? How do you explain away the one person you know who doesn't quite fit the stereotype you hold? How do you view rich people? Do you see them as greedy and ruthless, or do you regard them as generous, hardworking and innovative? What do you think your role as a man is? If a man thinks that sowing his wild oats is a mark of manhood, he will leave many fatherless children and devastated women in his wake.

How do you see God? As a sadistic puppeteer gleefully working the strings that control humanity, or as a loving Father who wishes only the best for you? Your whole life will be influenced by what you think, and more importantly how you think.

It really is worth taking the time to order your thoughts correctly. Whether you choose to do this or not, your thoughts will determine for example, who you marry, how many kids you have, which neighbourhood you live in, how much money you have in the bank, the kind of relationships you enjoy, how long you live, and so on. I have seen beautiful young women going out with and sometimes marrying the worst losers you ever saw, simply because the women in question thought they weren't worth much, and consequently gave themselves wholly to the first bum that showed an interest in them.

So ask yourself the question, where did my thoughts in this area come from in the first place? They may have been influenced by parents or friends, books you read or films you watched. They may have been borne out of your own experience. Unfortunately for many of us our thoughts are passed onto us unwittingly as we watch other people participate in the game of life. We watch on the sidelines cheering on football players who earn more in a week than some of us will earn in our entire lives and embrace their opinions on matters wholeheartedly. We sit in front of the telly and get dating and marriage tips from actors who aren't exactly the best role models. All around us, things are clamouring for our attention, and what we do pay attention to will eventually affect how we think, and in time, how we act.

I call thinking the lost art. Because of the busy lives we lead, very few people take the time to sit down and just think. Consequently many of the decisions we make are half-baked and result in at best average results, and at worst total disaster. Regardless of how busy you are, let this maxim guide you always: If you are too busy to think, you are too busy. Thinking is not a waste of time. I think it was Victor Hugo who said, "A man is not idle because he is absorbed in thought. There is a visible labour and there is an invisible labour."

Is it possible to achieve success without paying attention to your thinking? Possibly. But chances are the success will be fleeting, and your lack of attention in this regard will catch up with you somewhere down the line. I don't mind admitting that for many years I was on the lookout for a quick way to get rich, a million dollar idea that would set me up for life in my own right. The only problem was I didn't realise that this kind of thinking was subconsciously influencing the kind of opportunities I was pursuing. If it didn't guarantee a quick return I wasn't interested. I don't think you'll be surprised to learn that most of these ideas never panned out, and my last condition was always worse than my first. That's a gentle way of saying that I lost a bucket load of my money and other people's money as well.

This is the kind of thinking that plagues many of those that play the lottery. They queue up faithfully week after week, and pay out a portion of the pittance they earned that week, and walk away with visions of someday owning that house on the hill, the latest sports car and an 18 hole golf course. Despite the fact that the odds are roughly fourteen million to one that they will actually win the top prize, and that they are more likely to be struck twice by lightning in their lifetime than win, millions of people go through this insane rigmarole week after week. Well the only problem is because they think this is the only way out of their current financial situation, they do not even entertain the idea of other opportunities and consequently remain in their broke state permanently. Am I saying only poor people play the lottery? I am sure some rich people do too, but I think you will find they do not regard it as their primary plan for wealth accumulation.

One day, on a whim I decided to find out for myself what it truly was that I thought about most of the time. So I decided that I would write down every thought I had, either positive or negative over a twenty four hour period. Before long I saw a very clear pattern developing. No points for guessing that most of what I was thinking was highly negative. Half the time, I was having mental battles with my wife in her absence, subconsciously sparring and preparing all of the arguments and counter-arguments that I would put forward should we have a real argument. Is it any wonder then that the real arguments would subsequently take place? My mind drifted regularly to previous hurts and angers, and I found myself rehearsing how I felt at that time. Before then I could never understand the link between what I was thinking and how I felt. I soon realized that those negative thoughts I was having were silently wreaking havoc on my physical body. Let's just say that from the day I discovered this truth for myself, I decided to guard more carefully what I thought.

But it is not enough just to decide not to think negative thoughts. The negative ones have to be replaced with positive ones. If you don't do this then you may possibly find yourself worse off.

> 'When the unclean spirit is gone out of a man, he walketh through dry places, seeking rest and findeth none. Then he saith, I will return into my house from whence I came out; and when he is come, he findeth it empty, swept and garnished. Then goeth he, and taketh with himself seven other spirits more wicked than himself, and they enter in and dwell there: and the last state of that man is worse than the first.' (Matthew 12:43-45)

Have you ever emptied a room or a closet, and noticed that before long it is full of rubbish again? The same applies to your mind. Unless you make a conscious effort to feed your mind with the kind of material you wish it to produce in abundance it will continue to revert to type, and give you a very negative harvest. Think of positive things, things that bring you pleasure, that remind you of good times in your past. Refuse to dwell on the bad.

'Finally brethren, whatever is true, whatever is noble, whatever is right, whatever is pure, whatever is lovely, whatever is admirable – if anything is excellent or praiseworthy – think about such things.' **(Philippians 4:8)**

Actually these concepts are not difficult to get your head around. The world we live in is inherently negative, and we are conditioned to view things in a negative manner. The news we watch is very rarely positive, and so we become accustomed to hearing of murders, deaths, rapes, and earthquakes, to the point where our minds become numb. When a child is born, it has no comprehension of negativity. All things are possible. However through experiences and the input of others, this innocent mindset is changed until eventually that child takes on the phobias, fears, and inadequacies of those around it, and creates a few of its own for good measure. Some people do not become thinkers simply because their memories are too good. They remember what it felt like to try that business idea and have it fail, so they'd sooner avoid that pain, and do nothing, than think through what went wrong, and keep moving forward.

Your thoughts can determine whether you become a success or failure in life. Remember, it is impossible to be successful in anything unless you believe that you can actually succeed. A huge number of people battle feelings of inferiority and they doubt themselves, and this hinders the achievement of their dreams. This inferiority can stem from so many different sources, but whatever the source, it manifests itself in an inability to achieve because you think that you are not as good as others, that you cannot achieve what they have achieved. It is a good starting point to try and find out where these feelings stem from before you can adequately deal with them. But also there are simple things that can be done to deal with these feelings. The only reason why one is plagued with feelings of inadequacy or inferiority is because that is what has been consistently fed to your mind. To begin to have feelings of security and confidence the nature of what has been going into your mind has to change.

No matter where you go or what you do, you live your entire life within the confines of your head. So many people have left country after country, in the vain hope that they will find a place where they will succeed. What they will usually find, after they've travelled across different time zones, and exhausted their money, is that they are stuck with themselves, and that a little work on themselves would have made all the difference. It is not a coincidence that whatever country you live in 3% of the inhabitants of that land own 97% of the wealth. How you think is a hundred more times important than where you live.

It doesn't take long before you find out how people think. A couple of minutes into any conversation, and you pretty much are sure who you are dealing with. Statements like, 'Oh money isn't important to me, or 'the government will take care of me', give you the idea of a person who has a skewed perspective of life. Don't rely on such a person to do anything of value for you, like investing your savings or giving you a tip on a 'hot stock'.

You and I are not only what we eat but we are also what we think. If we spent as much time examining how we think and what we feed our minds, as we do examining what we eat can you imagine how different our lives would be? In the same way that physical food is required for physical growth, we need to feed and thus determine the health of our minds. Invest time in reading material that will force your mind to grow.

Thinking is like loving and dying. Everyone must do it for themselves. Don't delegate responsibility for your life to others because you are too lazy to do it yourself. This is the mentality of a loser. The average man never really thinks from end to end of his life, but mouths off clichés that he heard from someone else. As far back as 1508 Leonardo Da Vinci said:

'Irons rusts from disuse, stagnant water loses its purity and in cold weather becomes frozen; even so does inaction sap the vigour of the mind'.

And Albert Einstein wrote:

'The world we have created is a product of our thinking; it cannot be changed without changing our thinking'.

Begin challenging your own assumptions. Your assumptions are your windows into the world. Scrub them off every once in awhile, or the light won't come in. That is why it is necessary to constantly read and learn. Oliver Wendall Holmes once said:

'The mind, once expanded to the dimensions of larger ideas, never returns to its original size'.

Constantly challenge what you know, and continue to develop your mind.

I am sure you have the picture by now. Thinking is a vital key to your success. Isn't it true that we can live without air for a few minutes, without water for about two weeks, without food for about two months? And yet we can live without any new thoughts challenging our old ones for years. As I often say, if you read you will succeed. Develop the habit of reading extensively, and meditating on the things that will improve your philosophy.

"This book of the law shall not depart from your mouth, but you shall meditate in it day and night, that you may observe to do according to all that is written in it. For then you will make your way prosperous, and then you will have good success." (Joshua 1:8)

I leave you with this sobering statement by Adolf Hitler:

"What luck for rulers that men do not think."

Lesson 2 – A man and his purpose

"It is finished......" **John 19:30**

The legendary inventor Thomas Edison had just come through a period of exceptionally hard work and even longer hours than normal. At dinner his wife said, You've been working too hard with no breaks. You need a vacation". But where would I go?" he asked her. "Think about where you'd rather be than any other place on earth", she replied. Edison thought for a few moments then said, "All right, I'll go tomorrow morning". The next day he was back to work in his laboratory. **Thomas Watson Jr, Father Son and Co: My life at IBM and Beyond**

Over the course of my life I have had the opportunity to meet and speak to hundreds of men. It still saddens me however when I recall how many of those men had no idea what their purpose in life was. Many said that if they had known when they were younger what they had been born to do, they would have lived their lives differently, and made different career choices also. It also amazed me how many of them were pursuing careers that were someone else's idea. A number of them were hugely successful in those careers, but there was still a gnawing sensation in their gut that they were building in the wrong direction. They still had so many questions that needed answering. What exactly is my purpose? Why am I here? Why was I born?

As men we have so many different ways of measuring success. How much money we have in the bank, how many women we have slept with (the NBA basketball great Wilt Chamberlain proudly claimed in his autobiography 'A View From Above' that he had slept with over 20 000 women), how much people admire and respect us. But God measures the success of our lives using a totally different yardstick – how well did you fulfil your purpose?

There have been so many books written to try and redress the anguish that men feel at not knowing their purpose some very good, some not so good. Where a lot of them fall flat is simply their lack of understanding of what purpose is, and where it comes from. In order for

7

anything to truly understand its purpose, it has to look to its creator for that answer. Trying to discover purpose in any other way is truly an exercise in futility.

Put simply, purpose is the reason why something exists. The inventor of any product can readily tell you the reason why he created that particular product. Henry Ford for example, produced the Model T because he wanted to make an automobile that was within the economic reach of the average American. Today, Ford Motor Company continues to fulfil this purpose, with the Ford range being among the world's most affordable and best-selling cars. Similarly, at 15 years of age, Louis Braille invented the Braille system because he wanted to help blind people all over the world learn how to read. And today, 9 out of 10 blind people use Braille every day in their working lives. And Buckminster Fuller, an average individual without special monetary means or academic degrees dedicated his life to finding out what an individual like him could do to improve humanity's condition that large organizations, governments, or private enterprises inherently could not do. In fulfilling this purpose, he wrote over 28 books, and more than two decades after his death, is still widely cited as a mentor by hundreds of hugely successful entrepreneurs and business people. Similarly, God in creating everything that He created had a specific purpose.

The Lord has made everything for His own purposes. (**Proverbs 16:4**)

We live in an increasingly complex society in which it has become sophisticated to deride any mention of, let alone belief in God. Heaven forbid that any educated person should believe that God created man, and that he actually had a purpose for doing so. I mean, we live in the Information Age where there is supposedly a logical, scientific explanation for everything, including the existence of man and his reason for being here. Anybody who talks about the reality of intelligent design as espoused in the Bible is dismissed as needy and ignorant. Man is told to discover his purpose from within, as he is the source of his own life.

Sadly, all around us we are faced with living proof that this humanistic philosophy, and a lack of belief in God's purposeful creation of man, has caused millions of people to go to their graves unfulfilled and bewildered at how meaningless life can be when purpose is unknown or misguided. Aleister Crowley, an ardent Satanist once famously dubbed 'the wickedest man in the world', and the man who coined the satanic doctrine, 'Do what thou wilt shall be the whole of the Law' is reported as saying despairingly on his deathbed, 'I am perplexed'. As well he might be. It is a tragedy to live your life and discover at the end that you were involved in vainglorious pursuits and other endeavours that were not in the original will of God for your life. Life without God really doesn't make any sense. The Bible puts it like this:

"What kind of deal is it to get everything you want but lose yourself?
What could you ever trade your soul for?" (**Matthew 16:26**)

Some people dabble in the occult world, looking to astrologers, palm readers, and even Ouija boards to help them reach into the spirit world and discover their purpose and gain direction for their lives. The story of King Saul has always fascinated me in this regard. When Saul was rejected by God as king over Israel because he persistently disobeyed God's directions, his life went rapidly downhill. On one occasion he became so desperate to find a way to deal with the problem of the marauding Philistines, he turned to a medium for counsel, asking her to call up the spirit of the prophet Samuel. His words here are particularly apt.

> *"I am bitterly distressed; for the Philistines make war against me, and God has departed from me and answers me no more, either by prophets or by dreams. Therefore I have called you, that you may make known to me what I should do."* **(1 Samuel 28:15)**

When as men we reject the will of God and His purposes for our lives, we open ourselves up to deception, distress, sin and ultimately death. We begin to grope around as one who is in the dark, hoping to find by chance a way out of our predicament. But God knows the purpose for every aspect of your life. He has a purpose for your job, your money, and your talents. Unfortunately, when one doesn't understand the purpose of a thing, abuse of that thing is inevitable. Many men don't understand the purpose of women for example, so they slap them around and treat them as second class citizens. Others don't understand the purpose of the church, so they use it as a social gathering, or as a nursery to pander to the whims of immature men. Just as the original purpose of the woman was as a joint heir with the man in establishing God's rule in the earth, and the original purpose of the church was to train the body of Christ to fulfil their individual and corporate purposes on the earth, so too the original purpose of God's creation of man was for him to be an integral part of God's family and rule the earth in partnership with his Creator.

> *'And God said, "Let us make man in our image, after our likeness and let them have dominion over the fish of the sea, and over the fowl of the air, and over the cattle, and over all the earth, and over every creeping thing that creepeth upon the earth."'* **(Genesis 1:26)**

Because of His acute understanding of our purpose as men, God has placed us on the earth for a specific time in which we are to see our purpose through. We often don't realize that we have a finite time in this life and that we are obligated to live effectively for God in that time. Methuselah lived to be 969 years old and yet all the Bible records about him is that he got married, had some kids and then died. Talk about a waste of 969 years! Jesus lived to be 33 and his ministry only lasted 3 years, but in all of history, no one before or after has had a more dramatic impact on the course of the world. We need to measure our lives not by how long we live, but how effectively we live out our purpose in those years.

The truth is, if you don't know your purpose, you have no real way of allocating your time, or using your money. You even find it difficult to wake up in the morning. It is quite easy to tell when a man doesn't know his purpose. He will change jobs, churches and even spouses on a whim, trying to find that which best satisfies him. But nothing does. Benjamin Disraeli once wrote,

> *"I have brought myself, by long meditation, to the conclusion that a human being with a settled purpose must accomplish it, and that nothing can resist a will which will stake even existence upon its fulfilment."*

One of the primary reasons a large number of men never achieve anything of significance in their lives is because they never settle on a purpose. They are, to coin a phrase, a wandering generality as opposed to a meaningful specific. They start projects and never finish them. They have children and never invest the time to bring them up properly. After the initial excitement of beginning something new, they quickly realize that they didn't have a passion for that thing in the first place.

Can you sum up your purpose in a single sentence? For many years I couldn't, and my life was characterised by a degree of enjoyment and success, but in real terms there was an acute awareness in me that every business I was involved in, every project, was simply a means to an end, and did not give me a true sense of fulfilment. Over time I came to discover what I had been created to do – to raise a family in the knowledge and fear of God; to finance the preaching of the Gospel, and to extend the Kingdom of God until the return of Jesus Christ. Once I discovered this purpose, my anxious and desperate unease ceased. Finally I had something to live for that was bigger than myself, and that would govern the decisions I made and the direction I went. I am so grateful that I found out my lane before it was too late..

Don't be misled. In pursuing your purpose, you will face huge challenges and obstacles. All of these are designed to make you lose focus and question whether you are able to achieve what you set out to do. You need to understand that you are already equipped with all the talent and the passion you need to get the job done. You are already a winner in the game of life. Now all you need to do is play out that reality.

"I can do all things through Christ who strengthens me." **(Philippians 4:13)**

Are you struggling to discover your purpose? Colossians 1:16 reminds you where your journey of discovery should begin:

'For everything, absolutely everything, above and below, visible and invisible....
everything got started in Him and finds its purpose in Him.'

It if often said that good is the enemy of best. And for many of us in good jobs, with houses in nice neighbourhoods and pretty spouses, our satisfaction with the good things that we have been blessed with is often the thing that limits us from aspiring to discover the true extent of why we are here. Beware of slipping into a comfort zone of accomplishment – there are many more levels for you to attain. You see, it is our failure to see the bigger picture that cripples us. We need to live our lives from an eternal perspective, knowing that our time on this earth is just the first chapter of a drama that will be played out for eternity.

"I glorified you on earth by completing down to the last detail
what you assigned me to do." **(John 17:4)**

You have to discover your purpose. It will never be presented to you on a silver platter. It will require a committed search, an intense study not only of your character, your temperament, your skill set, but of the Word of God, so that you can get the answers you need from God himself. The greatest place of fulfilment in life is in the purpose of God. Our aim in life should be to discover the thing that God has called us to do, because that is where His power lies in wait, to transform us into creatures capable of feats beyond our wildest dreams. Too often we make our own plans and then expect God to bless them. But there are plans that He has laid for us even before He laid the foundations of the world.

'Many are the plans of a man's heart, but it is the purposes of God that will prevail'. (**Proverbs 19:21**)

I remind you again that you were created for God's pleasure, to dominate, and to rule the earth in the same way that God rules the heavens, in a partnership literally authored in heaven. That means if God has called you to be an entrepreneur, an attorney, a doctor, a teacher, your operating effectively in that area is part of you fulfilling that mandate to dominate in cooperation with Him. When we live apart from God assuming that all we have is our own, including our lives, we display a level of ignorance that left unchecked may result in our untimely demise.

'Then He told them a parable, saying, 'The land of a rich man was fertile and yielded plentifully. And he considered and debated within himself, "What shall I do? I have no place in which to gather together my harvest". And he said," I will do this: I will pull down my storehouses and build larger ones, and there I will store all my grain or produce and my goods. And I will say to my soul, Soul, you have many good things laid up, enough for many years. Take your ease; eat, drink, and enjoy yourself merrily". But God said to him, "You fool! This very night the messengers of God will demand your soul of you; and all the things that you have prepared, whose will they be?" So it is with the one who continues to lay up and hoard possessions for himself and is not rich in his relation to God, this is how he fares. (**Luke 12:16-21**)

You see, there is something about knowing your purpose that causes you to overcome all obstacles and refuse to give in to the temptation to quit when things aren't going right. Even your inspiration is tied to discovery of your purpose. Many men feel uninspired and limited by their lack of resources only because they don't have a big enough why. A well known philosopher once said, 'He who has a big enough why can bear any how'. Our job is not to concern ourselves unduly with how we will achieve our purpose, but to first discover that purpose, and then the rest will be revealed in time.

In your heart you probably know exactly what your purpose is, but fear and doubt limit you. For many men it is the challenge of making ends meet that causes them give up on their dreams and become mired in just getting by. Do not confuse your job with your purpose. There will be times when you need to do things that do not seem to fit in with your life's purpose, but they are noble in themselves because there is dignity in work.

'The appetite of the labourer works for him; for the need of his mouth urges him on.' (**Proverbs 16:26**)

Take the time to work out your purpose in great detail. God is intensely detail oriented, we should be too.

'Is there anyone here who, planning to build a new house, doesn't first sit down and figure the cost so you'll know if you can complete it? If you only get the foundation laid and then run out of money, you're going to look pretty foolish. Everyone passing by will poke fun at you: 'He started something he couldn't finish.' (**Luke 14:28-30**)

Be sure to write down your purpose, pulling it down from the unseen world where it was conceived, into the physical world where it will be accomplished. Keep clarifying it, expanding it, and keep growing in the process. Remember that even with a clear purpose, you will occasionally be distracted and uninspired. Whatever you are involved in, do not forget to ask yourself, 'How does this help me fulfil my purpose?' Learn to do something towards your purpose everyday, regardless of how insignificant it may seem. If you yearn to be a great speaker, read daily on how the greatest orators honed their craft. And once you discover your purpose, spend most of your time on it. So often we spend our time on low priority tasks that have very little potential for changing our lives.

I know my purpose, I live it, I love it.

Inspired people do inspired things. But before you get inspired, you need to get an understanding of who you are. A lack of identity results in a lack of purpose. As a man you were made in the image of God, an exact duplicate in kind. Show me a man who knows Whose he is and I will show you a man who knows his purpose in life. The two are inextricably linked. Satan convinced Adam and Eve that if they ate of the forbidden fruit, they would become just like God. He knew that if he could cause confusion in this important area, he could distort their purpose. And because they did not understand that they were already like God, they fell prey to his deceit. Satan tried to do the same with Jesus, but Jesus knew exactly who He was and why He had come to the earth:

'For this purpose, the son of God was manifested, that he might destroy the works of the devil.' **(1 John 3:8)**

He knew He was the son of God, and He knew He had come to the earth to destroy the works of the enemy. He accomplished this first of all by dying on the cross at Calvary, putting an end to poverty, sickness and disease and death and secondly by investing three years of His life in His disciples, teaching them the fundamentals of the Kingdom of God, doctrines that enabled them to literally turn the world upside down in no time at all. Discover for yourself who God says you are. If you don't know your purpose, someone else will determine it for you. And anything you don't decide on purpose will be decided for you.

Remember, it is possible to be successful in the sense of accomplishing amazing things and still fail to fulfil your life purpose. You can speculate about what your purpose is, or you can delve into the word of God and find out definitively.

'Weary yourself not to be rich; cease from human wisdom.' **(Proverbs 23:4)**

Live your life on purpose, not by default.

Lesson 3 –
A man and his perseverance

'They may trip seven times, but each time they will rise again…' **(Proverbs 24:16)**

"Victory belongs to the most persevering." **Napoleon**

"When you get into a tight place and everything goes against you, till it seems as though you could not hang on a minute longer, never give up then, for that is just the place and time that the tide will turn. **Harriet Beecher Stowe**

"It's a little like wrestling a gorilla. You don't quit when you're tired, you quit when the gorilla is tired." **Robert Strauss**

Sir Winston Churchill took three years getting through eighth grade because he had trouble learning English. It seems ironic that years later Oxford University asked him to address its commencement exercises.

He arrived with his usual props. A cigar, a cane and a top hat accompanied Churchill wherever he went. As Churchill approached the podium, the crowd rose in appreciative applause. With unmatched dignity, he settled the crowd and stood confident before his admirers. Removing the cigar and carefully placing the top hat on the podium, Churchill gazed at his waiting audience. Authority rang in Churchill's voice as he shouted, "Never give up!"

Several seconds passed before he rose to his toes and repeated: "Never give up!" His words thundered in their ears. There was a deafening silence as Churchill reached for his hat and cigar, steadied himself with his cane and left the platform. His commencement address was finished.

Being a man has never been more challenging. The weight of expectation from family, friends, and even society can often feel overwhelming. If the truth be told, it is often tempting to throw in the towel, to cave in and quit. And this applies regardless of what stage of life you are at.

When you are younger, there are the exacting demands of what seem to be never ending classes and exams, or the pressures of making the football team. As you get older, you are faced with the added challenges of pursuing a successful career, and raising a family. And in your twilight years, as your strength wanes and old friends and relatives pass on, there may be a very real sense of despair, wondering whether there is any point in going on. Whichever category you fall into, the reality is that trials will litter your way, and knowing this will help you to prepare for the trying times when they inevitably arise. Jesus put it this way:

"I have told you these things, so that in Me you may have perfect peace and confidence. In the world, you will have tribulation and trials and distress and frustration; but be of good cheer, take courage; be confident, certain, undaunted! For I have overcome the world. I have deprived it of power to harm you and have conquered it for you." **(John 16:33)**

Having the ability to persevere in the pursuit of your goals and dreams is what will distinguish you from the millions of people who give up at the first sign of trouble. Many quit on their marriages the minute challenges start. Or run out on their children when the financial strain becomes unbearable. Or take their own lives when their businesses fail and they are faced with social ruin and ignominy. It needn't be so. Whether your goal is to raise a successful family or to become a multimillionaire, along the way you will need to become well versed in the art of perseverance – refusing to quit when that seems to be the best option. As the saying goes, there is no traffic on the extra mile.

Do you realize the enormous cost of success? It is a price I have paid repeatedly over the years. I never bought into the idea that I would get anything easy. Whenever I found myself staring at the remains of another failed business, I would always remind myself of the great achievers I had read about or knew personally who overcame seemingly insurmountable obstacles to reach their goals. And I would pick myself up, learn my lessons and start over.

It doesn't matter where you go, the rules remain the same. Everyone wants to succeed. Why then is it that so few do? I think I know the answer. They persevered when everyone else had given up. Think of Thomas Edison, the great inventor who eventually managed to make the electric light bulb after nearly 10,000 failures. And the challenges of other greats such as Marie Curie, Helen Keller and Mario Lemieux are well chronicled. It is impossible to fail at something unless you give up on it. Nelson Mandela persevered in his belief that one day his country would be freed from the oppressive yoke of apartheid and he lived to see that day.

What will you do? Will you persevere and see things through? Or after meeting rejection or difficulties will you quit? Being able to soldier on in the face of great impossibilities and being willing to keep focused on the attaining of your goal are the hallmarks of the truly great. Every one of us faces our own storms. Whether it is a single mother bravely taking on the world and fending for her kids in the midst of abject poverty, or a professional athlete coming to terms with a career ending injury, those who refuse to give in must eventually succeed. Many of those around you will question your sanity, and recommend you give up. 'Follow the path of least resistance' seems to be the bastion call of the masses. If you are to ever rise above average you have to ignore the advice of the naysayers, and listen instead to that small unerring voice within you that tells you that you were created for greatness and that your hope is not misplaced. Many men start great things – very few see them through.

So failing at something is not the unpardonable sin. The fear of failure makes minnows out of men. Our greatest glory will never come from having never failed, but, having tasted the bitter pill of failure, still forging ahead towards our destiny. It has been said that difficult things take a long time, impossible things take a little longer, and that certainly rings true in the case of Peter J. Daniels, the Australian mogul who was illiterate until the age of twenty six, failed in his first six business enterprises and went on to create a huge empire. There is something truly inspiring in the stories all around us of men and women who have stared failure in the face, and yet refused to give in to its debilitating grasp. Calvin Coolidge, the 30th president of the United States is reported to have said,

> *"Nothing in the world can take the place of persistence. Talent will not;*
> *nothing is more common than unsuccessful men with talent. Genius will not;*
> *unrewarded genius is almost a proverb. Education will not; the world is full*
> *of educated derelicts. Persistence and determination are omnipotent."*

Failure holds so much fear for us as men but it is more the fear of failure than the reality of failure that is the real scare for most. We are conditioned to not aim too high just in case we fail, and to be realistic in our expectations. But the bane of society surely has to be the achievement of easily attainable objectives. The ability to persevere in the pursuit of great dreams is the stuff of legends and what distinguishes us from the many who have no real desire to be above average. The reality is we have failed so many times in so many things, but we have conveniently forgotten.

So it is with where you are now. The only time you become a failure is when you remain mired in the mud with the rest of the hogs. Being able to wash off the mud of temporary defeat and soldier on with your vision will guarantee your success. You may have to change a few things, make a few adjustments here and there, but you cannot give up on your dreams. There is a course for you to finish. Finish it.

I am reminded in this respect of the words of the apostle Paul to his protégé Timothy:

> *"I have fought a good fight, I have finished my course,*
> *I have kept the faith."* (**2 Timothy 4:7**)

One of the most difficult times in life is when you are in the middle of the journey between what God promised you and the manifestation of that promise in your life. There is an African saying that warns that the burden of whatever you are carrying feels heavier when you are about to arrive at your destination. It seems that just when you think you are there, all hell conspires to convince you to drop your load and give up on your dreams.

The story of David is probably the most endearing in this regard. Anointed as the next king of Israel at the tender age of sixteen, the next few months in David's life are simply amazing. He kills the giant Goliath, is betrothed to the king's daughter and has the women in the city singing his praises:

"And the women responded as they laughed and frolicked, saying, Saul has slain his thousands, and David his ten thousands." (1 Samuel 18:7)

It all seems too good to be true. But then circumstances begin to conspire against him in earnest. Saul develops an eerie and demonic dislike of David and determines to kill him. David has to leave the king's court, is estranged from his best friend, and spends the next decade on the run, at times having to feign madness to avoid certain death and having to put up with the surliness of fools like Nabal.

But things come to an unnerving head when David and his men return to their camp at Ziklag and discover that the Amalekites have raided it and taken away all their women and children. David's men are so distraught that they grieve until they no longer have the strength to weep. But sorrow soon turns to anger and they turn on their leader wanting to stone him. One can only imagine David's state of mind at this time. But he demonstrates the incredible resolve of one who knows that whatever God has promised him must inevitably come to pass.

'..but David encouraged himself in the Lord his God…And David enquired of the Lord saying, "Shall I pursue after this troop? Shall I overtake them?" And He answered him, "Pursue: for thou shalt surely overtake then, and without fail recover all."' (1 Samuel 30:6-8)

David obeys God and gets back everything he had lost and more. But the most significant aspect of this story is often overlooked, by even the most ardent scholars. At the exact moment that David is facing insurrection from his men, Saul is falling on his sword in Mount Gilboa and the kingdom is being transferred into David's hands. How tragic it would have been then if David had decided at this critical juncture to throw in the towel and give in to the overwhelming emotion he was obviously experiencing. How many times have you given up at the very moment that your victory was knocking at your door?

It is worth bringing a word of balance in this regard. If you are involved in activities that have not produced any fruit for a protracted period of time, then you need to take a long hard look at what you are doing to see whether you need to change tact somewhat or whether you simply need to ditch those activities for more productive endeavours. Perseverance in and of itself will not guarantee success. You may be building in the wrong direction and be involved in activities you are not gifted to carry out. Be honest with yourself and do not substitute fantasy for legitimate work.

*'He who cultivates **his** land will have plenty of bread, but he who follows worthless people and pursuits will have poverty enough.' (Proverbs 28:19)*

God expects us to produce results in whatever we put our hands to and if those results are not forthcoming it might be time to channel your energies elsewhere.

'And he told them this parable: A certain man had a fig tree, planted in his vineyard and he came looking for fruit on it but did not find any. So he said to the vinedresser, See here! For these three years I have come looking for fruit on this fig tree and I find none. Cut it down! Why should it continue also to take up the ground to deplete the soil, intercept the sun and take up room?

But he replied to him, Leave it alone, sir just this one more year, till I dig around it and put manure on the soil. Then perhaps it will bear fruit after this but if not, you can cut it down and out.' (Luke 13:6-9)

The key issue to keep in front of you at all times is what God has said to you. There is something about having God's Word on a matter that gives you the fortitude to succeed notwithstanding the inevitable challenges you know you will face.

"I know thy works: behold I have set before thee an open door, and no man can shut it: for thou hast a little strength and hast kept my word, and hast no denied my name. Behold I will make them of the synagogue of Satan…to come and worship before thy feet, and to know that I have loved thee." (Revelation 3:8-9)

Never give up.

Lesson 4 - A man and his failures

I've missed more than 9,000 shots in my career. I've lost more than 300 games. Twenty-six times I've been trusted to take the game-winning shot and missed. I've failed over and over and over again in my life. And that is why I succeed. **Michael Jordan**

I think and think for months and years. Ninety-nine times, the conclusion is false. The hundredth time I am right. **Albert Einstein**

A man meets a sage in the road. The man asks the sage, "Which way is success?"

The berobed, bearded sage speaks not but points to a place off in the distance.

The man, thrilled by the prospect of quick and easy success, rushes off in the appropriate direction. Suddenly, there comes a loud "Splat!!!"

Eventually, the man limps back, tattered and stunned, assuming he must have misinterpreted the message. He repeats his question to the guru, who again points silently in the same direction.

The man obediently walks off once more. This time the splat is deafening, and when the man crawls back, he is bloody, broken, tattered, and irate. "I asked you which way is success," he screams at the sage. "I followed the direction you indicated. And all I got was splatted! No more of this pointing! Talk!"

Only then does the sage speak, and what he says is this: "Success is that way. Just a little after the splat."

No one likes to fail. The very word strikes fear in the hearts of most men. And in an attempt to avoid failing in their endeavours, many do not even try. Success on the other hand is an intoxicating word. It evokes images of pleasure, being feted by your nearest and dearest, receiving respect and honour. And yet much success comes as a result of having tasted the bitter pill of temporary defeat.

Sometimes we fail because we are not fully equipped or knowledgeable about what we set out to do. Many of my early business ventures failed spectacularly because what I had was a burning desire to succeed, but none of the skills to make it happen. And yet my failures taught me more than I would have learnt by being an armchair critic, looking on and commenting on, but not truly participating in the game of life.

We have to change our perspective on what we perceive to be failure. True success comes for example in being able to look at problems and see the answer. We grow in the process, and discover our areas of weakness and our positions of strength.

Every time we make a mistake we have an opportunity to learn something new. Indeed failure is a natural part of life. Driving a car for the first time involves a cacophony of errors. A jerking car, sweaty palms, a nervous instructor. And yet just beyond these failures lies the smooth propelling of the same vehicle to an intended destination. As much as we wish we could learn all of life from reading about it in an instruction manual, there are some things you will have to learn by doing. The magic really is in the doing.

Failure is not an end in itself. No one admires the abject failure who resigns himself to life on the sidelines as a result of his failures. Rather it is a means to an end. Failing at something doesn't mean that you are a failure, and many cannot make the distinction between the event and the person. Just because you fail at a task doesn't make you a failure. No, true success comes from understanding that the setbacks you suffer, the lessons learned, and your determination to constantly grow and improve are the bedrock of lasting victory.

Conventional wisdom suggests that to succeed you must be very deliberate and try to anticipate everything that can possibly go wrong. But that only results in 'analysis paralysis' where you are so busy analysing everything that can go wrong, you end up doing nothing, and the opportunity passes. Actually, you need to double your failure rate. If you are not failing, it is a sure sign that you are not actually doing anything. Despite the best laid plans, many things will not work out the way you expected them to.

We lose when we choose to follow the path of least resistance in an attempt to avoid failing, and in consequence we become minnows when we were destined to be giants. Let's be honest. It is not easy to accept the kicks that life seems to relentlessly aim at your posterior. When you have motivated yourself by realizing that you deserve better for your life, it seems that all the forces of nature, people included, conspire to convince you that you are wrong. You apply for jobs and receive one letter of regret after another. You decide to reorganize your business affairs and do everything by the book and very soon you are treading water financially. But the miracle of life is that there is a place beyond this time of temporary pain that most will never discover, where the agony you have endured is rewarded with pleasure that was previously inconceivable.

> 'Don't drag your feet. Be like those who stay the course with committed
> faith and then get everything promised to them'. (**Hebrews 6:12**)

We spend so much time trying to cover up our failings that we fail to take on board the lessons that would launch us to our next level. David desperately tried to cover up his affair with Bathsheba, but this only resulted in the death of two innocent people and a storm of trouble in his household for many years afterwards. And yet in his humble submission to God, David reveals the awareness that one discovers more about himself at times of great failings than when everything is going along swimmingly:

'Wash me thoroughly from my iniquity and cleanse me from my sin. For I acknowledge my transgressions and my sin is ever before me. Against you, only you have I sinned and done this evil in your sight….Behold, you desire truth in the inward parts: and in the hidden part you shall make me to know wisdom. Purge me with hyssop, and I shall be clean: wash me, and I shall be whiter than snow. Make me to hear joy and gladness; that the bones you have broken may rejoice'. **(Psalm 51:2-7)**

We fail so often, many times despite our best intentions. We promise ourselves that we will treat our wives better, but in the next breath we are involved in an all out war with them, and we don't know how it came about. We vow that we will handle our money better, and then in a moment of weakness we spend beyond our means and have to pay for those excesses for months and even years afterwards. And yet unerringly the commitment to continuous improvement ensures that if we refuse to give up we will see the end of our faith.

'No matter how many times you trip them up, God-loyal people don't stay down long; Soon they're up on their feet, while the wicked end up flat on their faces'. **(Proverbs 24:16)**

The paralysis that comes with failure is emotional not physical, but it might as well be physical, because once we are paralysed mentally the war is over, and we cannot win. Pessimism in your circumstances and in other people is no reason for you to convince yourself that you will fail. Sir John Templeton's hugely successful investing strategy for example, is based on investing at 'the point of maximum pessimism'. When everybody believes that no good can come out of your failures and that you are doomed to a life of frustration and mediocrity, that is the time to become even more focused and determined to overcome the challenges that lie before you. It is often said that no one ever erected a statue to a critic, and words have never rung truer. It is those who are in the battle ring of life that have the opportunity to win the fight, and not those who are content to sit around and carefully dissect each and every point where you went off course. Be prepared for criticism. The road to success is littered with the corpses of the many that gave up at the first hint of resistance from those around them. Don't become one of them.

Every failure is the foundation for a larger success. The stories that enthral us and get us truly pumped up are very rarely the ones where success came naturally and fairly easily. Rather we become emotionally involved in those tales where the hero had to fight back from the brink of tragedy and disaster to win. Life does not always give us what we want. But we have to develop the mindset of a warrior, recognizing that a fighting and indomitable spirit is what will lead to unending success.

'From the days of John the Baptist until now, the kingdom of heaven has been forcefully advancing, and forceful men lay hold of it'. **(Matthew 11:12)**

Stress, negativity, and depression come when we have failed. We lose our zest for life and become consumed with trying to figure out what went wrong. Self evaluation is important, but the past has gone, and is but a distant memory. Instead, all around you are the endless possibilities that are your future, and you can create whatever future you want by embracing these wonderful opportunities and creating on the canvas of your imagination the very thing you want.

Do not be dismayed when you fail. Rather recognize that every failure is an opportunity for you to tap into reserves of strength and resolve that you didn't even know you had. On the other hand if you choose to wallow in the misery that failure inevitably brings, you will just become another soon to be forgotten footnote in history.

'If you faint in the day of trouble then you are a poor specimen.' **(Proverbs 24:10)**

As in every other area of your life the one thing that guarantees that you have it in you to pick yourself up when you fail miserably is that you serve a God who cannot fail. Do not be intimidated by your circumstances but embrace every obstacle knowing that He will help you pull through. Be encouraged!

'Be strong and of a good courage, fear not, nor be afraid of them: for the Lord thy God, he it is that doth go with thee; he will not fail thee nor forsake thee.' **(Deuteronomy 31:6)**

Marianne Williamson – A Return To Love

Our deepest fear is not that we are inadequate.

Our deepest fear is that we are powerful beyond measure.

It is our light not our darkness,

that most frightens us.

We ask ourselves who am I

to be brilliant gorgeous , talented and fabulous?

Actually, who are you not to be?

You are a child of God

Your playing small doesn't serve the world.

There is nothing enlightened about shrinking

so that other people won't feel insecure around you.

We were born to make manifest

the glory of God that is within us.

It's not just in some of us; it's in everyone

And as we let our own light shine,

we unconsciously give other people

permission to do the same.

As we are liberated from our own fear,

Our presence automatically liberates others

Lesson 5 – A man and his children

A child arrived just the other day,
He came to the world in the usual way.
But there were planes to catch, and bills to pay.
He learned to walk while I was away.
And he was talking 'fore I knew it, and as he grew,
He'd say, "I'm gonna be like you, dad.
You know I'm gonna be like you."

And the cat's in the cradle and the silver spoon,
Little boy blue and the man in the moon.
"When you coming home, dad?" "I don't know when,
But we'll get together then.
You know we'll have a good time then."

My son turned ten just the other day.
He said, "Thanks for the ball, dad, come on let's play.
Can you teach me to throw?" I said, "Not today,
I got a lot to do." He said, "That's ok."
And he walked away, but his smile never dimmed,
Said, "I'm gonna be like him, yeah.
You know I'm gonna be like him."

And the cat's in the cradle and the silver spoon,
Little boy blue and the man in the moon.
"When you coming home, dad?" "I don't know when,

But we'll get together then.
You know we'll have a good time then."

Well, he came from college just the other day,
So much like a man I just had to say,
"Son, I'm proud of you. Can you sit for a while?"
He shook his head, and he said with a smile,
"What I'd really like, dad, is to borrow the car keys.
See you later. Can I have them please?"

And the cat's in the cradle and the silver spoon,
Little boy blue and the man in the moon.
"When you coming home, son?" "I don't know when,
But we'll get together then, dad.
You know we'll have a good time then."

I've long since retired and my son's moved away.
I called him up just the other day.
I said, "I'd like to see you if you don't mind."
He said, "I'd love to, dad, if I could find the time.
You see, my new job's a hassle, and the kid's got the flu,
But it's sure nice talking to you, dad.
It's been sure nice talking to you."
And as I hung up the phone, it occurred to me,
He'd grown up just like me.
My boy was just like me.

And the cat's in the cradle and the silver spoon,
Little boy blue and the man in the moon.
"When you coming home, son?" "I don't know when,
But we'll get together then, dad.
You know we'll have a good time then."

Harry Chapin – Cats in the Cradle

Earlier I mentioned the statistic that the average father spends about 23 seconds a day speaking to his children. Is it any wonder then that our families are in such a mess? A father should be a provider, a leader, an encourager, a source of wisdom. And when he doesn't fulfil any of these roles, his children naturally gravitate towards others who fill in for him, often with very negative results. Unlike sitcom fathers who are able to solve any problem under the sun in 30 minutes, which includes adverts, many of the conundrums that face our children today take a lot longer to deal with, and as real life fathers we carry the responsibility for providing much needed guidance to our offspring.

The dynamics of a man's relationships with his children change so much with each passing year. From being totally reliant on you for their every need, to them finally being in a position where they are able to not only take care of themselves but also be of immense value to you with their own unique perspectives and insight, the changes take place rapidly, and require rapid adjustment. But my job became that much easier when I thought about it not so much from the perspective of trying to answer every single question that may arise, but giving you guidelines, footprints if you like, that would make your job that much easier.

As our children make the many transitions that mark the period between childhood and adulthood, we have to make sure that we make those transitions with them. This is a source of real frustration for young people particularly as they feel babied and disrespected. Respect, contrary to what many cultures teach, is not a one way street with it flowing from child to parent. It flows in turn from a parent to a child, with the parents treating their children as unique individuals. The Bible tells children to honour their parents, but in the same breath admonishes fathers not to frustrate their children.

> *'Fathers, do not exasperate your children; instead, bring them up in*
> *the training and instruction of the Lord'.* (**Ephesians 6:4**)

The real difficulty with our children is that when they are young, they experience many of the same emotions that adults do. Pain, anger, depression, excitement and grief, are just some of the wide spectrum of emotions experienced by all regardless of age. A child will experience these feelings, and not be sure how to deal with them. Even as issues such as sex, drugs, and depression rear their head, we must have the wisdom to help them tackle these heady and often confusing issues.

There is sage advice that goes thus – have compassion for the young, the middle aged, and the old, because you have already been or someday will be one of them. And yet when it comes to our children we seem to conveniently forget what it was like to be that age. Have you forgotten what it felt like being forced to wear that ugly sweater to school by your mum, knowing that all the kids would laugh at you? Or walking up to the prettiest girl in school, and having her laugh at your fumbling advances to your eternal chagrin? Surely we would make better fathers if we took the time to put ourselves in our children's shoes, and identify with the real challenges they go through.

All fathers at some level, me included, have tried to foster on their children a degree of perfectionism, expecting them to behave just right, and look just right, so that they can be held up as the perfect trophy children. Let's be clear - there is nothing at all wrong with striving for excellence in your children. There is something distinctly wrong however with measuring your child up against a standard they could never hope to attain. It is said a perfectionist takes pains to make sure that everything is just right, and then goes about giving those pains to everyone else. Maybe that is the problem. Perhaps in a noble effort to try and make sure that our children never go through the problems we went through, and make the mistakes we made, we try and orchestrate every aspect of their lives. Somewhere along the line we need to learn the value of unconditional love – to love our children regardless of whether they ever become a grade A student or make the football team. If your goals for your children are unattainable, the inevitable result is they will give up on them and even become rebellious. Our children are not trophies, but individuals with different goals, skills, and dreams, and we should never forget that.

Do we value performance over attitude? Is it more important to us for our sons to score the winning goal than it is to see them demonstrate grace and dignity in defeat? Much of the yob culture that plagues our society today is a direct result of our inability to handle things we don't like gracefully. If something doesn't go our way, someone must have done us wrong, and we demand our pound of flesh.

All children should get their identity from their fathers. When a father runs out on his family, he leaves them without his name and without an understanding of who they are. The sense of belonging that we give our children is key to them subsequently developing and becoming who they were meant to become.

'And a voice from heaven said, "This is my Son, whom I love; with him I am well pleased."' **(Matthew 3:17)**

It must be remembered that in this well known piece of Scripture, God's statement of love and ownership of His Son came before Jesus had ever performed a single miracle, fasted a signal day or done any other act worthy of commendation. It was based purely on the heart of a Father and the love that naturally flows to those who belong to Him.

Many fathers leave their children a generous financial inheritance. But I truly believe that the most precious gift a man can give his children is the love he has for their mother. I have spoken to grown men who today reflect sadly that they never saw their fathers kiss their mothers or even hug them. That they still talk about it years later, gives you an indication of the importance of these seemingly insignificant gestures. I learnt this lesson many years ago and decided that I would unfailingly give this gift to my children. Sure, sometimes they looked a little embarrassed when they saw us fawning over each other like two lovesick teenagers. But deep down they loved it! In a crazy sort of way it seemed to make everything else work. And that was especially important in the early lean years when we were just starting out.

Because we understand that our children are a gift from God, we should naturally recognize that since He gives us the children, He naturally has a vested interest in their well-being and upbringing. In the same way that He created us for a purpose, He created them with a specific purpose in mind, and we have a responsibility to help our children discover that purpose and seek God on their behalf concerning the direction we ought to take in bringing them up. We often tell our children that they can become anything they want to become in life. But that is not true. They can become everything that God created them to become. God's plan for our children is no less significant than the plans he has for us as their fathers.

We need to be consistent with our children. To love them consistently, and not on the basis of their performance. To be there when we promised we would. To punish them when we have promised to do so. A lot of our inconsistency in this regard has to do with laziness. You come in from work tired, and little Johnny is engaged in the very thing you told him not to, but because you are exhausted, you let it slide. The next time it'll be an employer or a policeman giving Johnny instructions, but because he has acquired a disdain for authority, he takes this into his adult life where the consequences are direr. Do not allow your children to sulk. This attitude may seem cute at first, but it quickly develops into an irritating and then dangerous character flaw.

Listen to your children. Have you ever been in mid-sentence talking animatedly to someone, and they look at their watch? Didn't you feel deflated? You'd be surprised at how often we do this to our children. And contrary to what you may think, they can tell when you are not listening to them. When you are involved in a conversation with them, don't baby them, asking meaningless questions such as 'how was your day'. Ask them loaded questions, such as, 'when you saw that happen how did that make you feel' giving them an opportunity to connect with you on an emotional level rather than on the cursory level most people communicate on. Take advantage of those teachable moments, when you get an opportunity to impart something of eternal value to your children in response to the many questions they have.

Forgive your children. The father's role as disciplinarian is unquestioned. What can usually be handled better though is the forgiveness aspect. When you have punished your child are you able to forgive them immediately, and hug them before they go to bed, or do you string out their forgiveness over a few days? It is well intentioned but misguided practices like this that cause our children difficulty in relating to the readily available forgiveness of God when they mess up. Often in a fit of self condemnation many children walk away from God, never to return. I believe that this is where erroneous teachings taught in Christian circles such as purgatory originate. To teach that God can forgive you immediately and unconditionally when you miss the mark seems too simple for the religious types who feel the need to pay in blood before they feel forgiven.

Teach your children about God. This is without question the greatest heritage that a man can give his children. Leave them a godly inheritance so that they may be able to walk with your God long after you are gone. It often seems as if we think that our Christian beliefs will somehow magically transfer themselves onto our children. Just look at Eli the priest in the Book of Samuel. His two sons ended up fornicating in the house of God, and he did nothing to stop them. I am pretty sure that he had done little in their formative years either to instruct them in the ways of God. It sends a shiver down my spine when I think about the many churches that make no real provision for their children and youth and cater for the needs of the adult members only. Refuse to give in to the humanistic influences of our present day that tell you that you cannot discipline your children, or instil godly beliefs in them. That somehow by doing so, you destroy their still developing psyche. The tenets you received from the Word of God concerning the way in which your children should be raised still remain in vogue today, despite the conflicting sentiments that are becoming increasingly popular.

> *'Train a child in the way he should go, and when he is old*
> *he will not turn from it'.* (**Proverbs 22:6**)

Whether we like it or not, there is a price to fatherhood, and I'm not talking about the financial cost here. Becoming a father can be one of the most nerve wracking experiences, but also one of the most rewarding. It forces you to examine your character, and work on your self like very few other things can do. It involves a great deal of sacrifice. But it is also an incredible opportunity to enjoy an experience that really is like no other. You look at your kids and wish they could remain young forever. But these are fleeting years which if not grasped and treasured will slip through your fingers never to be enjoyed again. The real challenges of establishing a career and balancing the financial and emotional needs of your children cannot be ignored. But balance is the key in this respect. Some men view it as a badge of honour to be working non-stop, bringing work home, missing mealtimes, football games and school plays. But it reeks of one of the most negative of human characteristics – selfishness. We get home and are too tired to read to the kids but will gladly spring up from the couch if an important client rings up requiring urgent assistance. Until your children become a priority they will continue to be a nuisance you impatiently tolerate.

The golden rule says simply that you reap what you sow. I cannot tell you the number of parents who regret never having spent time with their children. As they advanced in age, and began to wish for more time with their children, the children were away busily living their own lives, and had little or no desire to be around their parents. And so the parents spend their last years in isolation, with the phones not ringing, the clients not calling round, and no grandchildren around to make those last years that bit special.

My wife once told me the story of one of her uncles, a very successful businessman who abandoned his family for the lure of another woman. He totally neglected his kids and had absolutely nothing to do with their upkeep, even though he could have done so quite easily. His ex wife and the children struggled dreadfully just to put food on the table. Well kids don't remain kids forever, and they all without exception grew up and became even more successful than their father had been. Their father's fortunes by this time had taken a turn for the worse. He had lost his new wife, made some poor business decisions and ended up losing all his money. He lived out the last days of his life in a tin shack- miserable, destitute and alone.

'He who brings trouble on his family will inherit only wind, and the fool will be servant to the wise'. **(Proverbs 11:28)**

There are many lessons to be learnt from him and others like him. Even if you have children from a previous relationship, they remain your responsibility. They need your input in their lives even more than before. You see, when a father abandons his children, he opens them up to the influence of all kinds of elements. The girls, already suffering from insecurity and a lack of self worth, and in a vain attempt to find a man to fill the void you have left, tend to overcompensate and often end up with men who destroy them even further. The boys go off also having lost out on your stable maturing influence, and become fully grown in body but immature in character and replicate your behaviour on other hapless victims.

So many men crave after positions in authority at work, on committees, and even in the church. Yet in God's eyes before a man is worthy of leadership in any arena, he must first demonstrate his capability on the home front. What sense is there in unleashing a half baked leader on people in the wider community when he has failed to demonstrate his ability in the arena that matters the most.

'He must manage his own family well and see that his children obey him with proper respect. If anyone does not know how to manage his own family, how can he take care of God's church?' **(1 Timothy 3:4-5)**

As patently unfair as it may sometimes seem, God holds the man ultimately responsible for the well being of his family. But he has also equipped you through His Word with all the tools you need to be able to tackle the challenges and inevitable lows that are part of being a father. After all He is the greatest Father ever. It is worth listening to what He has to say.

Lesson 6 – A man and his mentors

'During the course of writing this book it struck me again and again that one world-changer has often been influenced or inspired by another. Lister was inspired by Pasteur. Jung was inspired by Freud. John F. Kennedy was inspired by Martin Luther King; Martin Luther King was inspired by Gandhi; Gandhi was inspired by Tolstoy. Tolstoy was inspired by Jesus. There is a kind of invisible chain of influences connecting them one to another **(Rodney Castleden – People who changed the world)**

Everybody has mentors. Everybody. The only thing is that most people aren't even aware of who or what mentors them. Some are mentored by movie stars, others by agony aunts, and some even by talk show hosts. Most have never even met their mentors. But when I talk about mentors, I am referring to the men or women who shape our destinies inexorably and inspire us to do and become what was seemingly impossible. I've never been big on the concept of the self made man – that mythical creature that succeeds all on his own without help from anyone. We all owe our successes in part to other people. An old school teacher, a boxing coach, a pastor, a parent. Having a mentor is often the only difference between success and failure.

The term 'mentor' has its origins in ancient Greek Literature. Legend has it that when Odysseus sailed the seas to join the war that was raging against the Trojans, he chose his friend Mentor to act as his son's adviser whilst he was away.

And mentoring works. In the early 1990's 959 boys and girls in eight US states were enrolled in the first national study of mentoring - the Big Brothers Big Sisters of America P/PV Impact Study. Half the children were assigned a mentor, the other half remained on a waiting list and served as a control group. After fifteen months the impact of having a mentor was measured. The findings were simply outstanding. Children and young people with a Big Brothers & Sisters' mentor were:

52% less likely to miss school

46% less likely to start using drugs

27% less likely to start using alcohol

33% less likely to hit someone

37% less likely to lie to their parents

Children and young people with mentors also reported improved self-esteem, better performance at school and improved relations with their families and peers.

Many of the world's most successful people have benefited from having a mentor. Freddie Laker mentored Richard Branson. Aristotle mentored Alexander the Great. And Lance Armstrong, a seven time Tour de France winner was mentored by Eddy Merckx, himself a five time winner.

Sometimes a mentor's death can cause irretrievable damage to the mentee. Most boxing pundits agree that when Cus D'Amato, Mike Tyson's legendary trainer and mentor died, it was a major turning point in Iron Mike's career, taking him from the high of being the most well known and outstanding boxer of his generation to the troubled and despairing lows that we have been witness to.

Everywhere I look the principle rings true. Even historically, there were many systems of mentorship, including apprenticing under the medieval guild system, and the discipleship system practiced by both Rabbinical Judaism and the Christian church. Other famous mentor-protégé pairs include Ezra Pound and T.S. Eliot, Benjamin Mays and Martin Luther King Jr, Paul of Tarsus and Timothy, and Andrew Carnegie and Napoleon Hill.

And yet so many view themselves as self sufficient islands, all knowing and all conquering. They refuse to serve others and learn their craft gradually, because they are in such a rush to make a name for themselves. So we have half baked politicians, leaders and teachers being unleashed on the unsuspecting public with devastating consequences.

> *'And if you have not been faithful in what is another man's,*
> *who will give you what is your own?' (Luke 16:12)*

I crossed paths with one of my first mentors in my first year of university. One morning, just before lectures, my friend Joe rushed up to me, excitedly waving the finance section of the paper in my face and pointing to a heading which read 'Local businessman enters into multi million dollar gold joint venture'. Even before I had finished reading through the article, Joe had already started laying out his plan. Instead of going to our first lecture, we sneaked off to the library, and quickly penned a letter to the businessman in question, telling him how inspired we were with his recent business success and how great it would be if we could meet up with him. We posted the letter and didn't think too much of it. A few days later, however, we got a letter from his personal secretary, asking us to contact her so we could arrange a meeting with her boss. Joe and I rang that very morning and got an appointment to meet up with him that Friday.

Well Friday came, and dressed up in our best clothes, we caught the bus into town to his offices. We were shown to his office, and he came in a few minutes later. He was dressed immaculately in a blue suit, white shirt and red tie, which I found out later was his signature look. But what I remember more than anything else was the intoxicating scent of his deodorant. That night was one of the best of our young lives. We spent the whole afternoon being regaled with stories of his business successes and failures, and were watered with a steady stream of food and drink brought in by a well groomed but appropriately reserved older gentleman. We left that afternoon with job offers, but more importantly an insight into the business world on an incredible level. Over the next five years, I worked for him at every opportunity and loved every minute. He was the first person to introduce me to the writings and speeches of Dr. Martin Luther King Jr, and we spent hours scribing his speeches. He taught me about how money worked in a very simple yet powerful way. He was a very generous man but he was also very astute in his dealings, and I marvel to this day how much of my decisions are still influenced by his unparalleled wisdom. In many ways this book owes its existence to him. He knew that there was a need to pass the baton of knowledge and character on to the next generation. He died 5 years after our first meeting, but his legacy lives on in me, and hopefully in those I will pass it onto.

So your success will be determined to a large degree by those who mentor you. There is dignity in serving those who are greater than you. But there is a cost to such service. It will require you to submit to the authority of another. There may be a financial cost. You may have to forego other opportunities that are enticing and lucrative. You will need to be so focused on catching your mentors' spirit that you are prepared to ignore the shortcomings that he or she may have. You are even prepared to accept that there will be many who criticize your singleness of purpose and try to sway you. But that is all part of the cost of transcending the daily grind in which most will operate throughout their lives and determining to live on a higher plane.

'If anyone desires to be My disciple, let him deny Himself, disregard, lose sight of and forget himself and his own interests and take up his cross and follow Me..' **(Matthew 16:24)**

Choose your mentors wisely. Because if you are truly following them someday you will become what they are and greater. If you do not want to become like them, find someone else to pursue.

The story of Elijah and Elisha is one of the most endearing examples of mentor-protégé relationships. Elijah had just had a supernatural standoff with the false prophets of Baal in which 450 of them were killed. The wicked queen Jezebel found out and issued a decree vowing that Elijah would be dead within 24 hours. Elijah fled for his life and hid in a cave railing upon God to kill him because he was the only man of God left and his circumstances were more than he could bear. But an angel came and sustained him and he went forty days in the strength of that food. God them appeared to him and gave him instructions, which included anointing Elisha to be a prophet in his place. So he left and found Elisha ploughing with his servants and he put his mantle on him. Elisha ran after him and asked for his permission to say goodbye to his family before he came with him, but Elisha testing him told him to do whatever he wanted. Here Elisha was faced with a dilemma. To hold on to that which was near and dear to him, or to reach for that which was greater than anything he had ever known. He made an instant decision.

'So Elisha went back from him. Then he took a yoke of oxen, slew them, boiled their flesh with the oxens yoke as fuel and gave to the people and they ate. Then he arose, followed Elijah and served him.' **(1 Kings 19:21)**

Because of his undying commitment to his mentor, Elisha completed the vision that had been given to Elijah by overseeing the overthrow of Jezebel and leading Israel into a time of unprecedented peace and prosperity.

> *'And when the sons of the prophets who were watching at Jericho saw him, they said 'The spirit of Elijah rests on Elisha. And they came to meet him and bowed themselves to the ground before him'.* **(2 Kings 2:15)**

Your greatest success in life will come when you find those whom God has connected you to, and serve them in a spirit of diligence and excellence. Only then will you become all you were created to become.

> *'In this world the kings and great men lord it over their people, yet they are called 'friends of the people.' But among you it will be different. Those who are the greatest among you should take the lowest rank, and the leader should be like a servant. Who is more important, the one who sits at the table or the one who serves? The one who sits at the table, of course. But not here! For I am among you as one who serves'.* **(Luke 22:25-27)**

As believers, we have the opportunity to learn from the greatest mentor of all, the Holy Spirit. His wisdom is available to show you how to live successfully and to avoid fumbling around in the dark hoping to stumble on the answers you need to make life work.

> *'But when He, the Spirit of truth comes, he will guide you into all the truth... and he will announce and declare to you the things that are to come, that will happen in the future.'* **(John 16:13)**

Lesson 7 – A man and his money

A dollar a day invested at various interest rates for 66 years

	% interest		Amount Accumulated
Hidden in a mattress	0%	=	$24,000
In a savings account	3%	=	$77,000
Certificates of Deposit	5%	=	$193,000
Corporate Bonds	8%	=	$1,000,000
Growth mutual funds	10%	=	$2,700,000
Aggressive growth funds	15%	=	$50,000,000
Real estate, businesses	20%	=	$1,000,000,000

(The One Minute Millionaire – Mark Victor Hansen and Robert Allen)

Money is an emotive subject. It can help to build relationships or be the source of strife and discord. It can bring great joy and cause untold sadness. It can be used to feed the poor, clothe the needy, and fund research into cures for deadly diseases. But it can also be used to sponsor terrorism, to manipulate the will of others, and to finance loose living. In reality however, money doesn't do any of these things. People do.

People have many different attitudes to money. Most of us can identify with the frustration of going out to work, getting a pay check, and then trying to stretch it to cover the myriad of bills and other living expenses that are part and parcel of every day living. Some believe money is evil, whilst others believe that it is the lack of money that is evil. Many take vows of poverty, with others doing everything they can to get their hands on money. Whichever way you look at it, it forms a key part of our daily lives, and you need to understand the laws that govern money and its acquisition. If you obey these, there is no limit to how much you can achieve.

Money is really just a magnifier. Whatever you are on the inside is manifested through your money. If you are a generous person, the more money you have, the more generous you become. If you are a philanderer, more money would simply enable you to carry out your activities in more exclusive locations.

Some people believe that all rich folk are only rich because they take advantage of other less fortunate people. And every time they come across a wealthy person they give them a disapproving look. But many people now understand that people become rich by serving the largest number of people and satisfying their needs. Car makers serve people by giving them a convenient means of transportation. Similarly, construction companies build homes to meet a demand for accommodation, and this nets them huge profits.

Working hard for money is not the only way to become wealthy. When most people need more money, they go out and work extra hours on their current job or get another one. The only problem with that however is that will likely have a negative impact on your health, your time spent with your family, and the general quality of your life. Not to mention the fact that you are more likely to be worse off because there will be additional taxes payable on your new found 'wealth'. And if your objective is to become wealthy, at this rate it would take an awfully long time.

Interestingly enough it is not just poor people who have an unhealthy attitude towards money. Some people who are rich are ashamed to have money. If a son for example never saw his Dad because he was always working, and he felt deprived in this area, he can sometimes view money as the cause of this deprivation and despise it, without understanding that his dad simply had an inability to balance his priorities. Or say a young man suddenly starts making more money than his Dad, in his very first job. This could cause him a degree of discomfort, and as bizarre as it may seem there are instances where a person will sabotage himself, rob himself of a promotion, or deliberately destabilise his business until his income goes down to a level he is comfortable with. What you believe about money will affect your relationship with it throughout your lifetime.

As with everything in life, the accumulation of money does not happen by accident. You need to focus on its accumulation. And as I mentioned earlier, there are laws or principles that govern its acquisition. Most men are too lazy to spend the time learning these principles, and would rather take a tip on some stocks from their equally broke friend, or spend their lunch hour in a lotto queue waiting for their lucky break. A more sure fire way of accumulating wealth is to understand these principles and set about applying them in your own life.

Many are under the misapprehension that God hates money, and that by being poor they are actually drawing closer to Him. But the Bible teaches that it is the love of money is the root of all evil. If you are willing to do anything to get money then evil is not far away. The Bible also teaches that if you are prepared to get rich at any cost you will not go unpunished. If you are willing to cheat on your taxes, defraud your company, steal from your neighbour just to get ahead, then you demonstrate your love for money. No, God wants you wealthy so that you can be a part of establishing His will in the earth.

Have you decided to become wealthy? What would you do with your wealth? Would you help out your parents financially, buy great gifts for your wife and children, travel the world, build hospitals? How much money do you want to get? It is remarkable how many times people talk about wanting more money, and yet they don't even know how much they want. Being specific about your financial goals is one of the most important steps to becoming wealthy.

You may be content with earning ten thousand pounds a year. Or you may want just enough for you, your wife, and your kids. On the other hand you may have a philanthropic streak, and want to spend your money on things that will benefit all humanity, such as hospitals, orphanages, or museums. Remember that life is best lived when it is lived for the benefit of other people.

How much would it cost you to live the lifestyle of your dreams? To be able to eat what you want and not what you have to eat based on how much it costs? To drive the car that you want instead of that leaky banger that your granddaddy left you? And have you ever given any thought to how much it would cost you to retire? Retirement seems a long way away for most, but the years have a habit of rolling by quickly. One of the reasons why most men work at jobs they hate well into their sixties, is because they have made no provision for their later years. And so at a time when you should be enjoying more relaxing activities, playing with your grandchildren, you are up at six in the morning to go to work in a job where your supervisor is the less than half your age, and your salary is the lowest its ever been. As your health deteriorates, and your medical expenses go up, you are forced to sell your home to pay for medical treatment, leaving behind no inheritance for your children and grandchildren, but a stack of bills and the resentment of those who will have to pay for the mistakes you made in your life. There have been so many scandals with pensions recently, and many retire expecting that their pension will cater for their needs only to discover that the funds have been misappropriated by the pension company, or that due to the ravages of inflation or poor investment strategies by portfolio managers, the funds available to you are insufficient to cater for your remaining years.

It is also vital to know where you are financially at any moment in time. For most facing up to this truth can be a very uneasy time, because the answers may not be to your liking. How much are you worth? How much do you owe? How much do you have in savings? How long could you live if you lost your job today? 70% of people would be bankrupt in 3 months if they lost their jobs, and the simple reason for this is because they live from hand to mouth, borrowing on next months salary to make ends meet this month. There is a better way. The greatest asset any man can have in building his and his families' financial future is financial literacy. Many men would sooner flip channels whenever something comes on their TV dealing with investments and turn over to a channel showing something a little easier on the mind. How many men read the back pages of the paper promising themselves that they will read the financial pages, but then lose interest when they discover that their football team lost the weekend derby? Financial literacy will give you the ability to understand money and build a financial empire of your own.

Reading consistently on money will be your biggest ally. Because if you understand how money works, you are less likely to lose your money in that deal that seemed (and was) too good to be true. There are many get rich schemes out there, but they are better dubbed get sick quick, because that how you'll feel when you lose your money, and you have to tell your family that you have gambled away your nest egg. The principles of investment show that even a minimum wage earner can become a millionaire in his lifetime if he invests wisely, and starts early. Sadly most of us fall victim to Parkinson's Law. Our expenses rise to meet our income. So if you currently earn ten dollars an hour, and you get a pay increase to twenty dollars an hour, chances are your expenses will rise to consume that increase and a little more besides.

It has often been said that if you are unable to save money, then the seeds of greatness are not in you. That may very well be true. A common fallacy is to assume that you will save when you make more money. The truth is that day will never come. It's no different from people who say they will start tithing when they earn more. If you can't be trusted with a fiver, how will you be trusted with five million. He who is faithful with little will be blessed with much.

Sadly, most, because of their unwillingness to learn, would much rather spend their time working furiously, instead of taking time to learn how to acquire money. And because a lack of knowledge is at the root of most of our problems, those with the knowledge end up making those without it pay for their ignorance. And nowhere is ignorance displayed more vividly than in the area of credit card debt. Young Jimmy carries a credit card around, and flashes it at every opportunity, to impress his friends. If that was all he did, that might be alright. But he also uses it to buy things that he can't afford. He waltzes into the mall, with his friends in tow, and his eyes fall on the latest gizmo, sneakers, jacket, and all of his good intentions go out of the window. He buys as much as his authorised limit will allow, not really considering whether he can pay the bill when it comes, but just picturing how good he will look in his new gear.

Refuse to be a consumer only. Build wealth by offering services that others are willing to pay for. Become an investor, not only in the financial markets of the world, but in the kingdom of God. Refuse to hoard your money, but use it as a means to serve humanity.

> *'There are those who generously scatter abroad, and yet increase more; there are those who withhold more than is fitting or what is justly due, but it results only in want.'* **(Proverbs 11:24)**

God has a plan for your financial prosperity just as much as He has a plan for every other area of your life. Invest the time to discover how to get hold of everything He has in store for you.

> *'Weary not yourself to be rich; cease from your own human wisdom'. (Proverbs 23:4)*

Lesson 8 – A man and his goals

In 1979 the graduates of the MBA programme at Harvard were asked, "Have you set clear, written goals for your future and made plans to accomplish them?" It turned out that only 3 percent of the graduates had written goals and plans. 13 percent had goals but they were not in writing. 84 percent had no specific goals at all apart from finishing school and enjoying the summer.

Ten years later, in 1989, the researchers interviewed the members of that class again. They found that the 13 percent who had goals that were not in writing were earning on average, twice as much as the 84 percent of students who had no goals at all. But most surprisingly, they found that the 3 percent of graduates who had clear, written goals when they left Harvard were earning, on average ten times as much as the other 97 percent of graduates put together. The only difference between the groups was the clarity of the goals they had for themselves when they graduated. **(Mark McCormack – What They Don't Teach You At Harvard Business School).**

Anybody who is successful in life is intensely goal oriented. That is because they know that without goals your life becomes aimless and fumbling. You drift, never accomplishing anything of significance. Jesus had a goal – to redeem men from their ignominious past by revealing God's kingdom to them and ultimately dying for them on the cross at Calvary. Despite the sheer horror and untold suffering He was aware lay before Him, He was determined to pay the price to see His goal accomplished.

> *'Now when the time was almost come for Jesus to be received up to heaven, He steadfastly and determinedly set His face to go to Jerusalem.'* **(Luke 9:51)**

Our era is awash with people of extraordinary genius and talent. But the reality is that a person of average intelligence, with clear goals will always run rings around a genius who is not clear on what he really wants to achieve. Just having a goal helps you to be able to order your life to accomplish it. Your goal will determine what you do with your money, the kind of friends you keep, how you spend your time. And it is almost as if nature, providence or call it what you will, comes to your aid to assist you in getting what you set out to achieve.

And it's not as if people don't know that they need to set goals. Every man wants to do well, to provide for his family, to have a successful career. I think the real problem has to do firstly with accountability and secondly with self discipline. If you have no written and clearly measurable goals, then you cannot be accused of having failed to achieve them in the event that you do fail. And having a goal means that you will have to forego many things that will not help you get to your destination. And it is these two factors in the main that cause most men to settle and make no real effort to set goals and accomplish them.

Not having a goal is a lot like driving around in a thick fog. Your progress is halting and uncertain and it takes longer for you to get to your destination. Defining your goals helps to clear the fog and allows you to get into gear and accelerate down the pathways of life.

So any plan is better than no plan at all. But another aspect we cannot ignore is the size of our goals. Our goals must stretch us, and cause us to become better fathers, husbands and citizens as we stride towards their accomplishment. They must have the capacity to change not just our lives, but the lives and destinies of those whom we are called to touch. Who can talk about the 20th century without mentioning Martin Luther King, Winston Churchill or Mother Theresa? Each had starkly different goals, but each one of them placed an undeniable mark on their generation. You must too. The German philosopher Johann Wolfgang Von Goethe once said 'To have more, you must first be more'. Refuse to settle for easily achievable goals. Set them in such a way that you will be forced to become better and better. This applies especially to the improvement of your character, which is the bedrock of all enduring achievement. Benjamin Franklin, a founding father and America's first millionaire started out penniless. But he had a propensity to be very outspoken and argumentative and he recognised that this was ruining his chances of long term success. He set a goal to develop virtues such as humility, temperance and sincerity. He became known not only as a renowned statesman but for being a man of inestimable character.

Let me ask you a question. How far would you be prepared to go to achieve your goals? Desire, passion and unflinching commitment are absolutely the key to getting what you want in life. Your desire has to literally consume you, and you must be willing to stake your very existence on your goal. It is easy to say you want to be rich, that you want to be happy. But those are not goals. They are wishes. And the last time I checked, the only person who had a genie giving him three wishes was Aladdin. A goal will demand relentless pursuit, not fanciful thinking. It may often force you to fly in the face of commonly accepted logic and convention. You may even have to endure mocking, ridicule and criticism. But if you really believe in your goal, you will use these negatives as a spur onto your next level. I always think of Noah being told by God to bring an ark and toiling away for 120 years in designing it, even though at that time no one had even seen rain. The same is true as you strive to live your life for God even though many around you mock your commitment and question your sanity. Remember it is your goal, your destiny. Ignore the so called experts. Albert Einstein one of the greatest minds known to man was sent home from school as a young man with a learning disability. Similarly Dr Albert Schweitzer's parents were encouraged to apprentice him to a shoemaker since it was felt that he could never achieve anything of significance. Both men earned doctorates before they were twenty. There are people whose primary assignment in life is to mock you and ridicule you, particularly when you strive to achieve that which is worthy of acclaim.

'First of all, you must understand that in the last days scoffers will come, scoffing and following their own evil desires. They will say, "Where is this 'coming' he promised? Ever since our fathers died, everything goes on as it has since the beginning of creation". But they deliberately forget that long ago by God's word the heavens existed and the earth was formed out of water and by water. By these waters also the world of that time was deluged and destroyed. By the same word the present heavens and earth are reserved for fire, being kept for the day of judgement and destruction of ungodly men'. **(2 Peter 3:4)**

Your goals are worthy of achievement regardless of what anyone thinks about them or you. If you wait for everyone to ratify the goals you set, you will be remembered for posterity only as a consensus seeker and not a man of destiny.

It is also possible to set goals, achieve them and then realise that the things you achieved weren't all they promised to be. You can make managing director, become a millionaire, or achieve worldwide fame and recognition. But success in and of itself cannot be enough. Your goals must be linked to your life plan. Think of them as incremental steps to you fulfilling your purpose. If you don't marry the two you may become successful as the world defines success, but never discover true happiness. Just ask Howard Hughes, the billionaire businessman who died a recluse, paranoid and unhappy, and despite having all the trappings of wealth, never lived out his purpose.

Think about it. Whatever you become in this life is up to you. You have it within you to create the future you want by choosing your goals and working them out regardless of the financial, social and other limitations you may be facing. There is no knight in shining armour that is going to come and magically transport you to your promised land. With the right goals it is possible to build your way to riches, fame and fortune. Conversely it is also possible to become decadent to the point where you are unable to feed and clothe yourself if you fail to clearly define where you are going. Don't blame others for where you are. Don't blame them when you fail to achieve your goals. Eleanor Roosevelt once said, "No one can make you feel inferior without your consent". You are in control of your future.

Start where you are. Set small goals and build on them. Break down your overall purpose into daily, weekly, monthly and yearly goals. If your goal is to lose two stone in weight, you could focus on losing half a pound a week. You would then accomplish your goal in three and a half months. Much easier than trying to do it all in one fell swoop. Sir Edmund Hilary is credited with being the first man to scale Mount Everest. Achieving this huge goal involved meticulous planning of smaller objectives and achieving them step by step. Similarly your success in life will be no more than the methodical accomplishment of a number of small achievable steps. Remember this when you feel overwhelmed by the enormity of your goals and vision.

So step out in faith and begin to set your goals. Don't procrastinate any longer. Start today.

Lesson 9 –
A man and his disciplines

'Feuerstein practices strict self discipline in both mind and body. He rises daily at 5.30 and either runs five miles or performs an hour of strenuous callisthenics. His daughter, Joyce, says he needles family members whom he deems overweight: "He bullies anyone who gains a pound." He monitors his pulse constantly, eats sparingly and says that he intends to live to be 120 – Moses's age. He subjects his mind to equal care: On even numbered days while exercising, he recites from memory an hour's worth of Shakespeare, Milton or the other English poets; on odd days, he recites in Hebrew from the psalms and the prophets, or from the Talmudic dictates on ethics. When he speaks in public, he does so without notes'. **(The story of Aaron Feuerstein adapted from Alan Farnham - Great Success Stories – Twelve Tales of Victory Wrested from Defeat).**

Contrary to popular opinion, we are not hapless victims of our circumstances. It is our choices that ultimately determine the direction that our lives take. Every single day you are given an opportunity to choose your path and it is these daily choices or habits that will be responsible for shaping your character and in time your destiny. It is Napoleon Hill who said, *'Our habits are fastened upon us by the repetition of our thoughts and acts'.*

> *'And he came to Nazareth, where he had been brought up: and as his custom was, he went into the synagogue on the Sabbath day, and stood up for to read'.* **(Luke 4:16)**

A habit is something you do so often that you do it without even realizing it. Have you ever driven home from work and not even noticed how your journey went? You've probably done the trip a thousand times and now you do it on autopilot. The same applies to a lot of our other behaviour patterns. Here's a habit a lot of men can relate to. You arrive home from work, plonk yourself on the couch, have your food brought to you and then watch TV until you pass out and your wife has to rouse you and take you to bed. Or you have a disagreement with your girlfriend or wife and instead of biting your tongue as you promised yourself you would, you give into

40

the temptation to trade insults, and before you know it you have a full scale war on your hands. Obviously these are examples of negative habits. And in fact most times when we talk about habits we use the word negatively to describe for example a drug habit or a binge drinking habit. But there is a positive side to habits and we will look at that in a moment.

But it is in the area of finances that our habits truly come to the fore. The habits we display in this regard have the greatest propensity to affect our lives beneficially or cause the greatest pain. Remember the movie "Groundhog Day," in which Bill Murray kept reliving the same day? Many people live their financial lives like that, repeating the same mistakes over and over again. But you don't have to be one of them. Spending without a budget, not tracking your spending, paying everyone else first and ignoring the cost of your borrowing, are all habits that will wreck your financial security. Small amounts of money spent without restraint are like the small leak in the dike that threatened the lives of an entire Dutch village.

I know many men whose desire is to retire rich. And yet when you look at their money habits they don't have a cat's chance in hell of doing so. They spend more than they earn plus some and they do not have a consistent savings or investment programme. You probably don't realize it, but your bad habits may be the one thing that is keeping you from achieving your goals and fulfilling your God given potential. They drain you of motivation, time and money. You delay doing the things that really matter. "I won't use my credit card for unnecessary purchases" you promise yourself. And yet in no time at all, you have bought a whole host of things that you don't really need, and really cannot pay for. Here too as in all the other areas of your life, you will have to change the way you think before you stand any chance of changing your habits.

Do you want to make dramatic strides in your financial life and overcome the bad habits that are holding you back? The Bible gives us a good starting point:

'Be thou diligent to know the state of thy flocks and look well to thy herds' (Proverbs 27:23)

Without realizing it, many men have strong feelings about money that come from childhood experiences and values. Many of these are based on fear and limited understanding and therefore do not set the right precedent for teaching the next generation the money habits that will enable them to succeed financially.

The financial education that our children need is generally not taught in the schools and consequently the responsibility for teaching good financial habits lies squarely on us. Teaching our children good money habits is about more than just preparing them for the world of work. Any time money is earned, spent, donated, shared, borrowed or saved there is a mindset that is operating in the background that is based on an understanding of, or lack of understanding of money habits. But the life long benefits of empowering them with good money habits make it well worth the effort. The children who are not taught these valuable lessons pay the consequences with lifetimes of financial uncertainty, distress, and even divorce.

It is a myth to think that you can control your bad habits. They are impulses and so whenever you try to control them, you only end up repeating the same tired patterns that are slowly destroying you. Bad habits have to be replaced. And replacing them with good habits will require diligence and a commitment to see through your objectives. A thing done once may make you feel good, but it is not likely to dramatically change your life.

There is an old story about a teacher who takes a bit of lightweight thread and wraps it one time around a student's wrists. He tells the class, "This string represents the power of doing something one time. Can you break the string?"

The student easily breaks the thread with a small flick of his wrists. The teacher then wraps the string around the student's wrists many times and repeats the challenge to break it. Despite repeated efforts, the lightweight thread is too strong to break.

His teacher says, "Now you see the power of repeated actions… habits. It takes more than mere willpower and personal strength to break them. It takes a change in the way you think about the problem."

When I was thirteen years old, I learnt what has now come to be known as a no exceptions habit. That meant that once you had set your goal you never allowed an exception to occur. At the time my single purpose in life was to develop rock hard abs. I wanted them so badly because every famous movie star or athlete I knew seemed to have them. So I asked my Dad to put me on a regimen that involved a series of exercises that I needed to do consistently every week. I stuck to it faithfully for about two weeks, but after a while the excitement of developing a six pack wore off and I gave up on the whole idea and never quite got that killer body.

For most men inconsistency is our worst enemy. To get to the top in any area of endeavour involves unrelenting and consistent focus and action. You cannot achieve success doing the right thing just the one time. It will take not only concerted effort, but concerted effort over a period of time.

I guess the worst thing about our bad habits is that the results of our choices don't show up immediately. Eating junk food twice a year is hardly likely to make a difference to your cholesterol level. But the same food eaten three times a week will wreak havoc on your life expectancy. The same thing applies to timekeeping. It may not make much of a difference if you are late for a couple of business meetings a year. But chances are this bad habit will happen more than just a few times and perpetuated over time it has the propensity to lose you not just business opportunities but professional credibility as well.

One of the best habits that I ever developed was the habit of reading. Even when I was younger I would hide myself away from everyone with a book in tow and read for hours on end. Over the years, my passion grew even stronger and I literally devoured all kinds of books. I have read thousands of books over my lifetime. Contrast this with the average man who reads less than one book a year. Reading opens your mind up to new ideas, to new and different ways of thinking. It is often said that all leaders are readers. It is one habit you cannot do without.

Think about the negative habits that you have. Are you always late? Do you let your paper work pile up for weeks and then discover that you have missed some important deadlines? Do you talk more than you listen? You must realize that it is possible for you to change all of these negatives into positives. Don't try and change all of them all at once; you may find yourself overwhelmed. If it is your intention to listen more than you talk, set it as a goal to monitor how long you talk for in each conversation you have and make sure that this time is consistently less than the time you spend listening. After a while it will become automatic, and you will be well on your way to becoming more personable and you will draw more people to you.

The Bible abounds with stories of people who had habits that were vital in ensuring their success. Jesus made it a point to go away and spend time with His Father consistently. Any wonder then that His ministry was characterised by uncommon power and authority. He was in the habit for example, of rising early.

> *'And in the morning rising up a great while before day, He went out, and departed into a solitary place and there prayed.'* **(Mark 1:35)**

Joshua, Moses' successor did the same thing.

> *'And Joshua rose early in the morning, and the priests took up the ark of the Lord.'* **(Joshua 6:12)**

One of the most endearing examples of disciplined living, and a life defined by excellent habits, was that of Daniel. From the time he was brought into captivity by the Babylonians he made it clear that he would not participate in any of their traditions that violated his own. He would not eat the rich food available to him and the other Hebrew captives from the kings' court, but chose instead to consistently follow a vegetable and water diet. But most admirable was his response to a royal decree that no man should make petition of a man or God except the king for thirty days. Daniels' enemies were aware that it was his custom to pray regularly to God and this was their way of laying a trap for him:

> *'Then the presidents and princes sought to find occasion against Daniel concerning the kingdom; but they could find none occasion nor fault; for he was faithful, nor was there any error or fault found in him. Then said these men, 'We shall not find any occasion against this Daniel, except we find it against him concerning the law of his God'.*

> *'Now when Daniel knew that the writing was signed, he went into his house; and his windows being open in his chamber toward Jerusalem, he kneeled upon his knees three times a day and prayed, and gave thanks before his God as he did aforetime'.* **(Daniel 6:4-5,10)**

Despite the obvious danger he knew he would find himself in, Daniel was not prepared to compromise his habits for any temporary reprieve. Talk about the no exceptions rule in practice!

Even the diminutive ant has something to teach us in this respect.

> *'Go to the ant, consider her ways and be wise: Which having no guide, overseer or ruler, provides her food in the summer and gathers her supplies in the harvest. How long will you sleep O sluggard? When will you arise out of your sleep? Yet a little sleep, a little slumber, a little folding of the arms to sleep, so shall thy poverty come as one that travels and your want as an armed man.'* **(Proverbs 6:6-11)**

Your habits have the biggest potential to change your life for the better. But they will not change until you change them.

Lesson 10 – A man and his friends

There once lived two men, called Damon and Pythias. They were both lovers of truth and integrity and in all the city of Syracuse they could find no one who upheld these principles so well as each other. Dionysius was at that time the ruler of Syracuse; he wielded complete authority and very often abused his power, for he was hot-tempered and imperious and anyone who angered him was put to death. One day he was informed that a young man named Pythias had been heard complaining against the cruelty of Dionysius; no one was allowed to criticise the ruler, and Dionysius condemned the youth to die. When Pythias learnt of his fate, he begged to be allowed to return home to set his affairs in order. "How far away is your home?" enquired Dionysius suspiciously, "and how may I be certain you will return?"

"My home is many miles distant," replied Pythias, "but I have a friend, Damon, who is willing to take my place while I am away".

There was a stir amongst the bystanders and a man stepped to Pythias's side. "I am Damon, my lord" he said. "I will give myself up as a pledge of my friend's return, and if any accident befalls him I will die in his stead." The tyrant was amazed by this generosity, and gave Pythias leave to depart, fixing on the day and hour of his return, and warning that he would not fail to exercise justice on his friend, if he did not arrive back in time.

The days passed and the morning dawned on which Pythias was to have been executed – still, Pythias did not appear, and the people of Syracuse said that Damon would surely be killed. Everyone was agreed in condemning his behaviour as rash and foolhardy; but Damon himself was the happiest man in the prison. He was filled with hope that his friend would not return in time, and he was led out to execution with a cheerful face. Dionysius had come to see him meet his death, and called out to him in mocking words. "So, Damon, where is your friend, of whom you were so confident? I fear you have allowed him to take advantage of your simplicity."

"It is impossible for me to doubt my friend's constancy," replied Damon. "Perhaps he has met with some accident along the way." At that moment a horse broke through the crowd, and Pythias, travel-

stained and weary, half fell out of his saddle, and ran to embrace his friend. "I am come in time," he gasped. "My horse was killed, and I could not find another. Thank heaven I am in time to save you!"

But Damon did not want Pythias to die. He pleaded with him to allow the execution to continue, and Dionysius watched in disbelief as each friend eagerly sought to give up his life for the other.

"Cease, cease these debates," he exclaimed, stepping forward and taking their hands. "I hereby set both of you free. Never in my life have I seen such loyalty; nor did I dream such a thing could exist. I beg you will accept my pardon and allow me to share in your friendship." **(Cicero, Treatises on Friendship and Old Age)**

The ancient proverb says "Tell me your friends, and I will tell you what you are". You are the sum total of the six people that you spend most of your time with. In fact it is often said you can guess a man's income to within a twenty percent margin of error by looking at how much his friends earn. Who your friends are will have a huge impact on who you ultimately become.

But even after you have formed your circle of companions, there is another duty you need to consider, and that is your conduct towards those whom you call your friends. Many men just like their younger counterparts are always unguarded in this respect. Be cautious and slow in choosing your friends. Do not allow what others expect of you to force your hand. There is much to be said for the considered choice. And when you have acquired a good friend, be firm and constant in your attachment. Do not abandon your friends without cause. Often young men in their rashness are too hasty in becoming intimate with every new person they meet, but within a few days or weeks they begin to perceive faults which they had not given themselves enough time to discern.

Also beware of relying too readily on the opinions and professions of your companions. That doesn't mean that you become surly or unduly suspicious. But you would do well to recall the experiences of the many who relied on their friends and didn't even live to regret it.

> *'Et tu Brute?' – Then fall Caesar. He dies.* **(Julius Caesar Act 3 Scene 1)**

Not all that glitters is gold. The human heart is deceitful, and those who really love you today may be different tomorrow. When you have tried a friend, and found him faithful, you may safely confide to him even your private thoughts. But take care that you are not deceived. *'The heart is deceitful above all things, and desperately wicked: who can know it?'* **(Jeremiah 17:9)**

Stick by your friends even when they are in any trouble. "A friend in need truly is a friend indeed." To forsake a friend in his time of calamity ranks among the basest of all human behaviour. Your Individual advantage and personal comfort have nothing to do with true friendship.. Even those who do not know God can teach us something in this respect. "The name of friendship," wrote Ovid, "touches the hearts of the very barbarians.

> *'As iron sharpens iron, so one man sharpens another.'* **(Proverbs 27:17)**

I remind you to be patient towards the faults of your friends. That does not mean you must love or condone their faults. Indeed in true friendship reproving and correcting one another are key elements. But do not abandon your friend for a few faults, or even for a great one, if he has been truly faithful, and if you are not put in danger by his faults.

'Better is open rebuke than hidden love. Wounds from a friend can be trusted, but an enemy multiplies kisses.' **(Proverbs 27:6)**

Be even tempered in all your friendships. An irritable man can never be a good companion, and his angry temperament is contagious, and you will soon share in his folly.

'Make no friendship with an angry man; and with a furious man you shall not go; lest you learn his ways, and get a snare to your soul.' **(Proverbs 22:24)**

I caution you to never do something wrong or illegal for the sake of friendship. What you compromise to keep you will eventually lose. If you seriously observe this rule, it will keep you from a thousand misfortunes. When Pericles, the influential statesman, orator, and general of Athens was asked by an intimate acquaintance to bear false witness for him, the great man answered, "I am your friend only to the altars," meaning, that he would go as far to help him as religion would allow.

Remember the great responsibility you have to share your faith with your friends. Many men have been converted by means of friendly admonition from those close to them. If our friends were sick, we would do everything in our power to heal them. How much more then should we try to ensure that their souls are saved from eternal damnation. A single word of affectionate advice sometimes does more good than many powerful sermons. And when a man professes to serve God, he ought to be neither ashamed nor afraid to open his lips on behalf of his Master's cause, regardless of the personal cost he may have to pay. You are the one that sets the bar for the rest of your friends. Refuse to reduce your standards of morality and excellence for the sake of fitting in. Many marriages have been wrecked because of men who compromised their integrity on a night out with the boys.

'A man that has friends must show himself friendly: and there is a friend that sticks closer than a brother.' **(Proverbs 18:24)**

A good friendship provides a safe place to share our deepest struggles. This is a level of friendship that most men will never experience, because they are afraid of being vulnerable. It takes time to build such relationships, but once established on mutual commitment and a foundation of trust, they are the tonic men need for the stresses of modern living.

As much as you love your wife and as good a friend as she may be to you, she can never be a substitute for the need that every man has to have male friends. With the temptations that assault us on a daily basis, it is absolutely vital to have strong men to walk through life with if we are to stay on a godly path.

'If one falls down, his friend can help him up. But pity the man who falls and has no one to help him up!' **(Ecclesiastes 4:10)**

Our manners, our habits, and our ways of thinking are gathered very much from the people with whom we associate. If you are comfortable in the company of the idle, the profane and the disrespectful, it is a sure sign that you are already corrupted, and you probably don't even realize it. And the longer you continue in their company the more harm you do to yourself. A Latin poet once said "No one ever became profligate all at once." The first steps are almost unnoticeable. When a man of good character first comes across ungodly companions, he is shocked by their behaviour. He is stunned when he hears them profane the name of God, and he runs from their presence. Their immodest conversation causes him to blush. When they tell lies wilfully, he is dismayed. However, after having been in their company for a while, both alarm and horror give way. He still dislikes their behaviour, but now his ears have become familiar to their language and he is comfortable in their company. And before you know it, in a vain attempt to fit in and show his companions that he is as fearless as they are, he is participating in their folly. At first he feels awful. But slowly this goes away. And with time he becomes just like his companions. How many men, both young and old have gone down this path?

'Blessed is the man that walks not in the counsel of the ungodly, nor stands in the way of sinners, nor sits in the seat of the scornful.' (**Psalm 1:1**)

One of the saddest disadvantages of keeping the wrong friends is often seen when the issue of a genuine relationship with God rears its head. When a man begins to turn his thoughts to discovering his true identity in God, often his friends turn upon him in ridicule. And all too often they are successful. Although most men won't admit it, they are more afraid of the scorn of their friends than they are of the wrath of God. They don't want anyone to know that they read their Bible or that they pray. And through this subtle ploy of the scoffers, millions have been drawn away from lives of true meaning.

"My son, if sinners entice you, do not consent—my son, walk not you in the way with them, refrain your foot from their path." (**Proverbs 1:10, 15**)

Enter not into the path of the wicked, and go not in the way of evil men. Avoid it; don't travel on it. Turn away from it, and pass it by." (**Proverbs 4:14-15**)

"Forsake the foolish, and live, and go in the way of understanding." (**Proverbs 9:6**)

Someone once commented to John Wesley, as he was starting his religious education, "You must either find companions—or make them." This is true of every one. It is not good for man to be alone. Even the beauty and serenity of the Garden of Eden was deemed incomplete until Adam had a companion, a helpmeet. You will have friends, and you will feel their influence. No man is an island. I can't even say with certainty what causes men to want to come together, but they do. And they need to.

When you make wise men your chosen friends, you put yourselves in the direct path of becoming wise and good. Relationships of this sort are invaluable in the formation of character. Their influence will weave a web around you, through which you will find it difficult to break, even if you desired to do so.

"He who walks with the wise shall be wise; but a companion of fools shall be destroyed." (**Proverbs 13:20**)

All the good things that your parents, teachers, and good friends have invested in you for years will disappear when you make friends with those who are fools in their own right. Lot chose the lure of Sodom and Gomorrah, was privy to its depravity and lost his family as a result. How different his life would have been if he had aligned himself more with his relative Abraham. No one ever rises to the fullest measure of excellence without friends. Conversely no one sinks to the lowest depths of evil without others urging him on.

A man who has trouble being faithful to his spouse is unlikely to continue in his ways if he is surrounded by genuine Christian men. Infidelity is a plant which does not thrive well by itself. Unfortunately there are others who seem to change their behaviour based on where they are. While in a church setting they are a whole new person. But once they are on their own they revert to type. Such a person usually lacks firmness and independence of character and falls in with the practices of his friends, even when he knows them to be wrong.

'Not forsaking the assembling of ourselves together as the manner of some is; but exhorting one another and so much the more, as you see the day approaching'. (**Hebrews 10:25**)

As a man you will be judged by the character of your companions. Birds of the same feather do flock together. Because of keeping the wrong company, it is possible for you to lose in an hour the reputation and character it cost you years of diligence to build. On the other hand when you seek the friendship of those who are wise, others take note of this and this will help to secure their respect.

We now have a friend that sticks closer than a brother. And yet how can we be His friend if we never think of Him? How can we truly be His friend if we do not cultivate thoughts of Him, or if we are ashamed or unwilling to speak of Him? A true friend loves at all times as He does. Our earthly friendships are often fraught with human shortcomings. But He is not limited by these infirmities. He is faithful to us regardless of what we do:

"You are my friends if you do whatsoever I command you. Henceforth I call you not servants for the servant does not know what his lord does: but I have called you friends, for all things I have heard of my Father I have made known to you" (**John 15:14-15**)

Lesson 11 – A man and his words

Well, I don't know what will happen now. We've got some difficult days ahead. But it doesn't matter with me now. Because I've been to the mountaintop. And I don't mind. Like anybody, I would like to live a long life. Longevity has its place. But I'm not concerned about that now. I just want to do God's will. And He's allowed me to go up to the mountain. And I've looked over. And I've seen the promised land. I may not get there with you. But I want you to know tonight, that we, as a people will get to the promised land. And I'm happy, tonight. I'm not worried about anything. I'm not fearing any man. Mine eyes have seen the glory of the coming of the Lord. **(Martin Luther King – I've been to the mountaintop)**

We have before us an ordeal of the most grievous kind. We have before us many, many long months of struggle and of suffering. You ask, what is our policy? I can say: It is to wage war, by sea, land and air, with all our might and with all the strength that God can give us; to wage war against a monstrous tyranny, never surpassed in the dark, lamentable catalogue of human crime. That is our policy. You ask, what is our aim? I can answer in one word: It is victory; victory at all costs; victory in spite of all terror; victory, however long and hard the road may be. For without victory, there is no survival. Let that be realized: no survival for the British Empire; no survival for all that the British Empire has stood for, no survival for the urge and impulse of the ages, that mankind will move forward towards its goal.

But I take up my task with buoyancy and hope. I feel sure that our cause will not be suffered to fail among men. At this time I feel entitled to claim the aid of all, and I say, "Come then, let us go forward together with our united strength." **(Winston Churchill – Blood, Toil, Tears and Sweat)**

If anyone does not stumble in what he says, he is a perfect man, able to bridle the whole body as well. Now if we put the bits into the horses' mouths so that they will obey us, we direct their entire body as well. Look at the ships also, though they are so great and are

49

driven by strong winds, are still directed by a very small rudder wherever the inclination of the pilot desires. So also the tongue is a small part of the body, and yet it boasts of great things. For every species of beasts and birds, of reptiles and creatures of the sea, is tamed and has been tamed by the human race. But no man can tame the tongue; it is a restless evil and full of deadly poison. With it we bless our Lord and Father, and with it we curse men, who have been made in the likeness of God; out of the same mouth come both blessing and cursing. My brethren, these things ought not to be this way'. **(James 3:2-5, 7-10)**

A man's life will rise no higher than the words he sits under. To this day there are men of all ages who reflect forlornly on the negative words they heard when they were growing up and how these affected them. 'You'll never amount to anything', 'you're stupid', or 'you're going to end up just like your dad', are all common variations of the kinds of words I am referring to. These often come from parents, teachers, pastors and other authority figures. And to a young man these words can cause untold damage. There are some who seem to cope better with negativity and words like this seem to simply roll off them like water off a ducks' back. But for most the mental recorder that plays relentlessly in their heads can cause them to perform at a level that is far below their God given potential. Conversely, there are many great men who trace their success to the influence and words of those who spoke into their lives and awakened the giant within. Donald Trump for example has spoken often about the enormous impact that Norman Vincent Peales' sermons had in arming him for the future.

If we have limited respect for and understanding of the power that words have, we run the risk of not ordering our own words to our advantage, and also being content to live under words that do not help take us where we need to go. Actually when you really look at it, the age old battle between good and evil is at its core a battle for words. God desires to sow His Word into the hearts of His people so that it can grow and produce a harvest of life. By the same token the devil, in typically nefarious fashion, tries to get his negative words to gain ground in the hearts of men which in turn produce death in all its forms.

With his mouth a man can lift up his voice and sing praises to his Creator. He can sing songs that encourage even the weariest heart. He can convince the damsel of his dreams to become his bride. But with the same tongue he can rail against God, he can pull down his neighbour and ravage his character, and he can scar his children irreparably with his unguarded words. We cannot underestimate the creative ability that we have been gifted with and must come to the realization that we can use this awesome power to harm just as much as we can use it to do good.

Someone once said that the greatest weapons in our arsenal are given free at birth, and so we don't realize how truly potent they are. The challenge of being mute is something that many will never have to endure. It represents a disadvantage that can only be overcome with great difficulty. In Hebrew culture it was popular to swear an oath by avowing that if the person making the oath was lying, then their tongues should cleave to the roof of their mouth. Indeed in many historical accounts, demons that afflicted people made them dumb, thereby reigning in the victim's innate ability to create with his words. And it is equally significant that in much of Jesus' ministry you see Him freeing people from this kind of captivity:

As they went out, behold, they brought to him a dumb man possessed with a devil. 'And when the devil was cast out, the dumb spoke; and the multitudes marveled, saying, "It was never so seen in Israel". (**Matthew 9:32-3**)

Words are vitally important. Moses complained to God that he wasn't up to the job of delivering the Israelites from the oppression of Egypt and Pharaoh because he was slow of speech and had a slow tongue. But God advised him to join forces with Aaron who was a fluent speaker, and assured him that he would be with them both:

'You are to speak to him and put the words in his mouth; and I even I will be with your mouth and his mouth and I will teach you what you are to do. Moreover he shall speak for you to the people; and he will be as a mouth for you and you will be as God to him'. (**Exodus 4:15-16**)

God places so much value on our words that He promised us that when we are fully submitted to Him, He would speak through us, even in difficult and life threatening situations.

'And when they bring you into the synagogues and to magistrates and powers, take no thought how or what thing you shall answer or what you shall say. For the Holy Ghost shall teach you in the same hour what you ought to say'. (**Luke 12:11-12**)

The Bible also tells us that God has exalted His Word above His name. That means that when we find His Word on anything, it is as good as money in the bank. On the other hand, when we dispute what He has said, we are actually calling His character into question. When the angel of the Lord appeared to Zacharias to announce the impending birth of John, who would come to be known as John the Baptist and herald the arrival of the Son of God, his scepticism in the face of God's Word caused the angel to strike him dumb. And for many months he was unable to speak until he fully acquiesced to this significant plan of God at which point he got his speech back.

'And his mouth was opened immediately and his tongue loosed and he spoke and praised God'. (**Luke 1:64**)

Without question our tongues are one of the single greatest assets we have at our disposal. When a man develops the ability to guard his words he guards his entire life from trouble. Death and life really do reside in the tongue and so each man often needn't look any further than his own mouth for the success he so desperately craves, or for the trouble he has created. Everything we see around us and even the things we do not see were created by God with His words. He imbued us with that same capacity. But used wrongly, words have capacity to do much harm. A word spoken at an inopportune moment can cause a fire that takes all the rains of heaven to quench. Potiphar's wife used all her guile and seductive ability to lure Joseph into sleeping with her. But when he would not, she decided to get even with him by telling her husband that Joseph had tried to force her into relations with him. You can only imagine the rage that Potiphar felt upon hearing of this treasonous act.

'When Potiphar heard the words of his wife, his anger was kindled. And Joseph's master took him and put him into prison...' (**Genesis 39:19-20**)

We betray our plans and our secrets with our words. And many times we allow people to know things about us that enable them to use that knowledge against us.

> *And his brothers said to him, 'Shall you indeed reign over us? Or shall you indeed have dominion over us? And they hated him yet the more for his dreams and for his words'.* **(Genesis 37:8)**

We speak so casually and yet when we begin to reap the consequences of these ill-thought out words, we genuinely seem surprised as if somehow there has been a miscarriage of justice. We lie, not realizing that when we speak deceit we align ourselves with the father of lies in whom there is no hint of truth. Speaking the truth is an integral part of developing the character that every man needs to have. There are not many things that God hates, but a lying tongue is one of them.

> *'There are six things the Lord hates, seven that are detestable to Him: haughty eyes, a lying tongue...'* **(Proverbs 6:16-17)**

It is not inconsequential that when satan tempted Eve, he called into question what God had said. After all, once you can cause doubt and confusion in the creation's mind about what the Creator has said, you immediately leave him or her on a very uncertain foundation.

> *Did God really say 'You must not eat from any tree in the garden'?* **(Genesis 3:1)**

Words can strike fear into the hearts of even the strongest men. Goliath repeatedly taunted Saul and his men and they were violently afraid. Despite the fact that he cursed them and their God, they were so intimidated by his threats that they refused to go out and fight him. Similarly when Jezebel got word that Elijah had called fire down from heaven and killed 450 of Baal's prophets, she sent out a chilling edict that had Elijah scurrying for his life and wishing he was dead.

> *'Then Jezebel sent a messenger to Elijah saying, "So let the gods do to me and more also if I make not your life as the life of one of them by tomorrow about this time."'* **(1 Kings 19:2)**

Without realizing it Jezebel unwittingly signed her own death warrant by vowing to eliminate Elijah and then failing to do so. Who was it who said that we are snared by the words of our own mouths? A short time later warrior Jehu presided over her gruesome death as the dogs of the city ate her flesh and licked up her blood.

Everything of significance that happens to us in our lives will stem from our words. The blessing was transferred from Isaac to Jacob through words. Even the awesome gift of speaking in tongues that allows us to have untainted communication with God makes use of words that we cannot understand without divine help and allows us to draw upon the wells of wisdom that so often lie dormant in the hearts of men.

Our success in life will not be determined by the volume of our words. Jesus admonished us not to think that we would get God to respond to our prayer just because we used many words in our prayer. Rather there is the need to ensure that our words are not couched in ignorance and unbelief, but carry the very power of God. Then they will get His attention.

And when you pray, do not keep on babbling like pagans, for they think they
will be heard because of their many words. Do not be like them, for your
Father knows what you need before you ask him. **(Matthew 6:7-8)**

Our words are a vivid reflection of what is going on in our hearts. There is a point in the Book of Job, where Job is so riddled with the emotional and physical pain of his turmoil that he sounds almost delusional. He embarks on the biggest pity party recorded in the Scriptures, expecting God to empathize. But listen to what God had to say:

"Who is this that darkens my counsel with words without knowledge? Brace yourself
like a man; I will question you, and you shall answer me. Where were you when
I laid the earth's foundation? Tell me if you understand." **(Job 38:2-4)**

After God has chided Job, Job begins to see the reality of his situation through God's eyes. And with that realization comes a change in his words.

'Then Job replied to the Lord: "I know that you can do all things;
no plan of yours can be thwarted... surely I spoke of things I did not
understand, things too wonderful for me to know."' **(Job 42:1-3)**

My prayer for many years has been that I would become proficient with each passing day in speaking how God desires me to speak – in accordance with His Word.

'Let the words of my mouth and the meditation of my heart be acceptable
in thy sight O lord my strength and my redeemer.' **(Psalms 19:14)**

But I didn't always think that way. When I first got married, I was a young whipper snapper with a fierce temper and a tongue to match. And the first couple of years of my marriage were very tumultuous. Each time we had a disagreement every negative word ever invented would drip from my lips. Even though I knew what the Word said about a soft answer turning away wrath and that in a multitude of words sin is not far away, I still allowed my emotions to hold sway. I'll never forget the time we had yet another argument, and for the first time I realized that my words were having no effect on my wife. It was as if she had steeled herself against anything I had to say to her. The only problem was that even afterwards, when in a lucid moment I would tell her that I loved her, those words didn't mean anything to her anymore. Staring the emotional loss of my wife in the face, I took a long hard look at myself and vowed that from that day forward I would never allow the cutting words that had reduced my wife to a shell of her former self to ever emanate from me again.

Let me remind you also of the dangers of allowing the words of the deceitful to chart your course through this life. How many men have lost themselves, having fallen prey to the words of seductive and immoral women, who rob them of their vitality, their promise and their lives?

'So she seizes him and kisses him, and with a brazen face she says to him, "...come let
us drink our fill of love until morning; let us delight ourselves with caresses. For my
husband is not at home, he has gone on a long journey, he has taken a bag of money

with him". With her flattering lips she seduces him. Suddenly he follows her as an
ox goes to the slaughter...until an arrow pierces through his liver; as a bird hastens to
the snare, so he does not know that it will cost him his life'. **(Proverbs 7:13-23)**

Everyone knows well the story of Samson, the mighty warrior who had a penchant for Philistine women. Delilah, at the behest of the Philistine leaders who wanted to destroy Samson, repeatedly asked Samson what the source of his strength was. He didn't look strong, but when the anointing came on him, he displayed the strength of ten men. When she first started asking him, Samson found the whole thing quite amusing. But after a while her persistence began to wear him out, and he told her the secret of his strength.

'And it came to pass, when she pressed him daily with her words, and urged
him, so that his soul was vexed unto death, that he told her all his heart and
said unto her, "A razor has never come on my head, for I have been a Nazirite
to God from my mothers womb. If I am shaved, then my strength will leave me
and I will become weak and be like any other man."' **(Judges 16:16-17)**

The Bible also cautions you that there are times when you mustn't take to heart the words that are spoken against you.

'Also do not take seriously all words which are spoken; so that you will
not hear your servant cursing you. For you also have realized that you
likewise have many times cursed others.' **(Ecclesiastes 8:21-22)**

Every man has the awesome opportunity to use his mouth to build a life of significance and prosperity. The sad reality is that if he fails to do so, the wisdom he has will be despised even by those he has helped.

'Now there was found in it a poor wise man, and he by his wisdom
delivered the city; yet no man remembered that same poor man. Then
said I, wisdom is better than strength; nevertheless the poor man's wisdom
is despised, and his words are not heard'. **(Ecclesiastes 9:15-16)**

When one has the good fortune of discovering those who have been placed in his life to empower him with their words, he must ensure that he pays whatever price is necessary to continue to allow those words to be sown in his heart. Often there will be many who will not place the same value on those words as he does, but this is one area where the opinions of others must not be allowed to predominate. The words may be hard to take, but often it is those words that you really need to hear.

'As a result of this many of his disciples turned back and no longer followed him. So
Jesus said to the twelve, "You do not want to go away also do you? Simon Peter answered
Him, "Lord, whom shall we go? You have the words of eternal life". **(John 6:66-68)**

And finally, I urge you to not be too quick in committing yourself to any course of action. You owe it to yourself to familiarise yourself with all the facts before you open your mouth and mortgage your future by speaking words that are not carefully considered:

> *'Do you see a man who is hasty in his words? There is more hope for a fool than for him.'* **(Proverbs 29:20)**

Lesson 12 – A man and his labour

Edward C. Barnes was a man of much determination but few resources. He was determined to ally himself with the greatest mind of his day, Thomas Edison. When he arrived in Edison's office unannounced, his poor appearance made the clerks laugh, especially when he revealed that he had come to be Mr. Edison's partner. Edison had never had a partner. But his persistence got him an interview with Edison, and the interview got him a job as a handyman.

Edison was impressed with Barnes's determination, but that alone was insufficient to convince him to take the extraordinary step of making him a partner. Instead Barnes spent years cleaning and repairing equipment, until one day he heard Edison's sales force laughing over the latest invention, the Dictaphone.

They said it would never sell. Why replace a secretary with a machine? But Barnes, the handyman, jumped up and cried, "I can sell it!" He got the job.

For a month Barnes pounded the New York City pavement on a handyman's salary. At the end of that month he had sold seven machines. When he returned to Edison, full of ideas for selling more machines all across the country, Edison made him his partner in the Dictaphone business, the only partner Edison ever had.

What made Barnes so important to Edison? The inventor had thousands of people working for him, but only Barnes was willing to display his faith in Edison's work and to put that faith into action. He didn't demand a fancy expense account and a big salary to do it either.

> *Barnes focused favourable attention on himself by rendering service far beyond a handyman's responsibility. As the only one of Edison's employees to render this service, he was the only one who uncovered such tremendous benefits for himself. (Thomas Edison's Only Partner – Napoleon Hill's Keys to Success).*

'He also that is slothful in his work is brother to him that is a great waster.' **(Proverbs 18:9)**

'He said therefore, a certain noble man went into a far country to receive for himself a kingdom and to return. And he called his ten servants and gave them ten pounds, and said to them "Do business till I come."' **(Luke 19:13)**

There is no greater enemy to self improvement and progress than laziness. An unwillingness to apply yourself to a task will paralyze even the noblest desire, and stifle every desire for advancement. If you are naturally lazy, you must resolve to overcome this flaw and do so with every fibre of your being.

The slothful man will always have a convenient excuse to fall on when he is asked to do something of value. There is always some obstacle when he is called upon to make any exertion. This attitude prevents him from attempting anything difficult or laborious. When requested to do anything, he always has something else to do first, which his previous laziness had left unfinished, or he has some other reason to give why he should not attempt it. The wise king Solomon put it this way:

"The slothful man says there is a lion outside—I shall be slain in the street!" **(Proverbs 22:13)**

As enjoyable as it may seem, laziness causes nothing but misery. The happiest and most fulfilled men are those who are the most active. That doesn't mean that they don't have periods of rest and relaxation. But it must be remembered that to fail to participate in useful work will cause you to stagnate in both mind and body. The saddest man is the one who has no work to do. Fulfilling labour is at its core an activity that is most invigorating.

A slacker on the other hand is one who has a static unenthusiastic air, and is unmotivated to apply himself in any area. The term was commonly used initially to describe men who were doing their best to avoid the military draft in the U.S. Today it could comfortably be used for the millions of men, both young and old, who somehow think that they can obtain great success in this life by only giving the minimum of effort.

Laziness is a great waste of one's existence. If you were to live to be seventy and you just wasted one hour a day, you would have thrown away three years of your life. And if we take it a step further and say that the hour is taken from the waking hours of your day, it would actually be calculated as six years of wasted time. Are you willing, by idleness, to shorten your life by six years? No? Then take care of the moments. Never fritter away time in doing nothing. Whatever you do, whether study, work, or play, enter into it with spirit and energy and never waste your time in purposeless activities. Whatever you decide to do, determine to do it well. For the harsh reality is that when you go to the grave, that opportunity to work as we know it will be lost.

"We must do the works of Him who sent Me while it is day. Night is coming when no one can work." **(John 9:4)**

The old adage says that 'all work and no play make Jack a dull boy'. You could just as easily substitute it with 'all play and no work makes Jack a mere toy'. The rich playboys of the world who are the envy of the many men who wish they could be in their shoes, soon lose their passion for life. The way we are wired, there is an incessant desire that burns in our bosoms to produce, and grow and develop. Once that desire is lost, all that remains is a life of ignominy and frustration and the steady descent to an early grave.

Labour is not just for the poor. There are men who think that just because their parents are wealthy, work is beneath them. Regardless of one's station in life labour is vital to help you develop your natural abilities. If a man is lazy, he will never discover the full meaning of manhood or accomplish anything of significance. A man who does not know how to work is half a man. His wealth or education can never cover up this glaring deficiency.

When Adam committed high treason and ceded control of the earth to his adversary satan, the curse he attracted meant that he would eat his bread in the sweat of his brow. Work which was intended to be a pleasure became burdensome and difficult. And for the many who are unaware of the redemptive work of our Lord in revoking that curse and restoring us to our original authority, there remains only a morbid fear of work, and a desire to live only for pleasure.

"I passed by the field of a sluggard, by the vineyard of a man lacking sense, and behold, it was all overgrown with thorns; the ground was covered with nettles, and its stone wall was broken down. Then I saw and considered it; I looked and received instruction. A little sleep, a little slumber, a little folding of the hands to rest, and poverty will come upon you like a robber, and need like an armed man." **(Proverbs 24:30-34)**

In Jewish culture, it was a strict requirement that every young man have keen knowledge of some form of labour. The apostle Paul for example, notwithstanding his membership of a wealthy family and being educated as a lawyer in the highest schools in the nation was also brought up to a trade as a tentmaker. And years later when he was set apart by the Master as an apostle, his tent making skills were of immense value to him as were his advocacy skills as a lawyer. Regardless of what occupation you desire to pursue, do not despise the practical knowledge that normal tasks will bring.

If you look down the annals of history you will discover that many of the greatest men that ever lived had an occupation that may not have seemed glamorous but was a necessary part of their preparation for roles of generational significance. King David was a shepherd. George Washington was a farmer. Jesus was a carpenter. The apostles were variously fishermen, lawyers, and tax collectors.

It was the Russian novelist and playwright Maxim Gorky who said:

"When work is a pleasure, life is a joy! When work is a duty, life is slavery."

And Thomas Carlyle, the 19th century Scottish philosopher, summed up this view in a speech in 1866, when he said:

"Work is the grandest cure for all the maladies and miseries that ever beset mankind."

Only a fool despises labour. But a man's work is not only necessary to make him a true man. It is also necessary to make him happy. Many long for the day when they will retire and think that they will be truly happy when they no longer have anything to do. The reality is that more than eighty percent of them will die within three years of retiring. Anything you do not use you will eventually lose.

If, then, you truly desire to be happy, you must cultivate the love of useful labour. This will give you independence of character and enable you to take care of yourself, without relying on the generosity or pity of others. It will save you from the temptation to surrender your independence, or commit any act of baseness or dishonesty for the sake of a living.

> *'And that you study to be quiet and to do your own business and to work with your own hands as we commanded you; That you may walk honestly towards them that are without and that you may have lack of nothing.* **(1 Thessalonians 4:11-12)**

For many men work is something they do to get a pay check so that they can then go on to do the things they really want to do. So they lumber through their working day, casting furtive glances at the clock and waiting for the stroke of the clock that signals the end of their toil. The minute they leave their place of employment, their demeanour is no different from that of a caged animal that has just been released into the wild. These men are the bane of their employer's existence. Every task they are assigned is either done shoddily or with the minimum effort possible. Such men will never be entrusted with the hearts of those in authority over them.

> *'As vinegar to the teeth and as smoke to the eyes so is the sluggard to them that send him.'* **(Proverbs 10:26)**

Even God gave instruction that there should be six days of labour and one day of rest. The way the vast majority live their working lives, one would be forgiven for thinking that one day of labour was the prescribed amount, with six days of rest and relaxation the acceptable norm. This breed of man is nothing new. Since time immemorial he has existed, living off his woman, his friends, or the state. A real man must not only understand the value of labour, but also recognise that if he refuses to participate in it, he forfeits his right to the benefits that it brings:

> *'For even when we were with you, this we commanded you that if any would not work neither should he eat.'* **(2 Thessalonians 3:10)**

The man who is lazy will describe for you in vivid detail the exact car he wants to drive, the kind of house he desires to live in, and the lifestyle he would like to enjoy. And that is as far as it goes. It is those who are diligent in their endeavours that shall enjoy the good that this life has to offer. Every desire of his heart can be fulfilled if he is willing to apply himself faithfully to his work. And yet despite this possibility many are unwilling to pay the price of disciplined labour.

> *'The sluggard will not plough by reason of the cold; therefore shall he beg in harvest and have nothing.'* **(Proverbs 20:4)**

Our work is not something we do just to pay the bills. God gave Adam the mandate to work before he ever gave him a woman, but more importantly before the fall. Work is not a form of punishment but a divinely provided means of giving expression to every creative ability that man possesses. The same mandate given to dominate the earth still remains in place today, and it is through our work that we are able to expand God's agenda and influence in the earth. Indeed the rewards we shall receive will be based on how effective we have been in accomplishing the work that was set out before us.

"I have glorified thee on the earth: I have finished the work which You gave me to do." **(John 17:4)**

"And behold I come quickly, and my reward is with me to give every man according as his work shall be." **(Revelations 22:12)**

Lesson 13 - A man and his health

"A wise man ought to realise that his health is his most valuable possession" **Hippocrates**

The average man can expect to be seriously or chronically ill for 15 years of his life.

The majority of men are too heavy for their health: 45% are medically defined as overweight and an additional 17% as obese.

The suicide rate among men is increasing. The rate has doubled among 15-24 year old men in the past 25 years.

28% of men still smoke

27% of men drink alcohol at a level that could be harmful to their health

31% of all male deaths under the age of 75 are caused by cancer, the second most common cause of death. Each year over 24,000 men of all ages are newly diagnosed with cancer and over 80,000 die.

Many men are affected by sexual problems. Recent American research suggests that almost one-third of men of all ages say they climax too early and nearly one-fifth of men in their 50's experience problems achieving or maintaining an erection.

Male Health Forum Statistics 2006

We have already established that there is a purpose for you being on this earth at this very unique moment in time. That you are here to carry out an assigned role that you are individually equipped to carry out. But be warned that you will not be able to truly fulfill your purpose without getting the greatest vigour, energy and fulfillment from your body. How many people do you know that have passed on before their time because they refused to treat their bodies as the temples that they were designed to be? The only thing that is worse than not fulfilling your destiny because you die prematurely, is being alive but being unable to do what you know you need to do because you have abused your body to the point that when you make demands of it, there is nothing left in the tank.

Too many men, young and old, are unable to perform at peak levels because they do not understand the needs of their bodies and how they can get the most mileage out of them. It's no different from buying a car and never quite getting around to servicing it and yet somehow expecting it to give you a consistently excellent level of performance. The golden rule in the area of health, as with every other area of life, is that you will invariably reap what you sow.

Everything in life has a natural rhythm. From the waves of the sea to the changing seasons. You too have a rhythm and in order to get the most out of your body you must understand its rhythm and balance. How well do you balance work with play, eating with fasting, and seriousness with humour? If you do not tune into your rhythm your body may well be so highly stimulated that you end up becoming stressed and subsequently find it difficult to operate at your peak.

Three of the greatest destructive forces are fear, anxiety and anger. They kill your enthusiasm, destroy your faith, blind your vision and blunt creative effort. Men need to invest in their mental health just as much as they do in their physical health. And yet most men are for all intents and purposes, walking zombies, going through the motions. The challenges of life have taken their toll on them and they have given up on their dreams and often they don't even know it. They are anxious about how to make ends meet, worried about whether they measure up to their peers, angry at their spouses, their circumstances and their bosses. And many of these concerns are manifesting themselves in physical problems such as hypertension, cardiac arrest, and various immune disorders. Most men are unaware that many of these ailments are either the product of mental distress or are greatly exacerbated by it. Be aware of the debilitating nature of fear and anxiety and make sure you do not allow them to wreak their evil on you.

When a man is angry, he will rarely admit that fear is often at the core of his anger. Fear of not measuring up to what society expects of him. Fear that he won't make good on all the promises that he made to his wife when they first met. Fear that God won't come through for him. Anger is of itself not a bad thing. Even the Word tells you to be angry and not sin. And often our inability or unwillingness to get angry is the reason we tolerate bigotry, injustice and prejudice in our societies. But fear must never be tolerated. Never. It makes minnows of men. And it devastates your mental and physical well being.

Whilst you're at it, avoid the negative emotions. Emotions are a wonderful gift from God that enable us to truly participate in life. So we cry with joy when we witness the birth of our children. We squeal with delight when we get good news. But no one benefits when we engage in envy, unforgiveness and strife. There is a reason we are admonished to refuse to countenance these. Not just because they are sin, but because they will literally kill you and hinder you from seeing God's goodness manifested in your life.

'He is conceited and understands nothing. He has an unhealthy
interest in controversies and quarrels about words that result in envy,
strife, malicious talk, evil suspicions.' **(1 Timothy 6:4)**

Food is another area that many men struggle with. The primary purpose of food is to supply the body with the nutrition it needs to keep itself in good working order. The body is a work of genius but it requires the right food to keep it working at its optimum level. Feeding your body with junk food, drugs and cigarettes might placate your hunger in the short term, but there will be a price to pay sooner or later. The statistics on worldwide obesity are staggering. For the first time in history there are more people suffering from obesity than there are those suffering from malnutrition. Avoid overindulgence in this area. King Stomach, to coin a phrase, is sitting comfortably and belligerently on his throne. But you have the power to dethrone him.

Always remember that a lack of control in one area of your life will have a knock-on effect on other areas also. It is vital that you educate yourself on the right things to put into your body, so that when you make demands on it, it is not running on empty. Remember too to never eat when you are angry, frightened or worried. Your body cannot cope with these emotions and still make use of the nutrition in the food for your benefit.

But it is not just the food that we put into our bodies that is of vital importance. It is also the many other socially accepted poisons that hold out the promise of unending pleasure that must be looked out for. Excessive drinking, the use of nicotine and recreational drugs are causing untold pain and suffering. I have never met any smoker who wasn't aware that their habit was potentially life threatening and at the very least would severely impair their quality of life. One only hopes that our concern for the well being of our fellow human beings will give us the mental stamina to deal with accusations of moralizing from the very people who need the most help.

Who has woe? Who has sorrow? Who has strife? Who has complaining? Who has wounds without cause? Who has redness and dimness of eyes? Those who tarry long at the wine, those who go to seek and try mixed wine. Do not look at wine when it is red, when it sparkles in the wineglass, when it goes down smoothly. At the last it bites like a serpent and stings like an adder. Under the influence of wine, your eyes will behold strange things and loose women and your mind will utter things turned the wrong way, untrue, incorrect and petulant. Yes, you will be as unsteady as he who lies down in the midst of the sea, and as open to disaster as he who lies upon the top of a mast. You will say, They struck me, but I was not hurt! They beat me, as with a hammer, but I did not feel it! When shall I awake? I will crave and seek more wine again and escape reality'. **(Proverbs 23:29-35)**

One of the events that would mark my life forever took place when I was in the sixth form. A friend of mine, Dapo, whom I shared a study with, together with a couple of other guys, was in the habit, like most young students, of bunking out of the halls late at night and going out to a local night club. At the time we all thought it was just a bit of fun, and looked up at Dapo with not a little respect and awe. What we didn't know however was that in addition to having a penchant for loud music and 'friendly' women, Dapo had also developed a craving for heroin. One night he slipped out of the dorm as normal and never came back. We woke up to the news that he had been discovered dead in the alley outside the club, having overdosed. Just another depressing example of how one can short circuit their lives by their own hands.

There seems to be an eerie unawareness of the consequences of our actions. Maybe it is because the consequences often come so many years after the event that we are unable to link the two.

When you are a frisky teenager you never stop to think about the reality of liver disease or clogged arteries. But when you are plagued with ailments of all kinds at a later age, the excesses of youth no longer seem as exciting.

It is an established principle that whatever you focus on will grow. If you do not make good health a priority, you will by implication suffer the consequences of your lack of attention. A cursory glance at the libraries of most men will usually reveal books on how to become a millionaire, how to succeed in investing, and autobiographies on other successful people - all excellent resources in their own right. They will very rarely however have a single book that educates them on how to improve and maintain high health standards. True success in life is composed of success in all spheres – financially, emotionally, relationally, spiritually and physically.

So make sure you get sufficient sleep. Your body needs time to rebuild and revitalize itself for the challenges of each new day. Insomnia is often caused when you fail to relax before going to bed and choose to take issues to bed with you. Different men need different amounts of sleep, but again be sure to know your own body and understand its individual needs. Our lives have never been more hectic than they are today but that is all the more reason to ensure that activity is tempered with planned periods of relaxation that will ensure that when you are working, you are able to do so at a peak level.

You will also need to engage in some form of physical exercise to keep your lungs and heart strong. Exercise is both mentally and physically stimulating and clears away any sluggishness you may be feeling as well as aiding your concentration.

Remember too that your mental health is just as important as your physical health. Refuse therefore to allow any unforgiveness to be in your heart towards anyone. Carrying grudges and unresolved angst against anyone is like drinking poison and hoping that someone else dies. It will rob you of your vitality, dull your passion for life, and ultimately may even kill you.

> *'Be gentle and forbearing with one another and if one has a difference against another, readily pardoning each other; even as the Lord has freely forgiven you, so must you also forgive'.* **(Colossians 3:13)**

Related to your health and just as important are your personal grooming habits. Manufacturers of products ranging from televisions to perfume invest a great amount of money in ensuring that the packaging for their particular product is well thought out and appealing to the potential customer. Equally it is important to understand that if you want to sell yourself to others, you have to package yourself appropriately. As pedantic as it may seem, however, people do make a judgment about you in the first four seconds of meeting you, and if the first impression is negative, then the chances of you turning it into a positive impression are very slim. And I am on very good ground when I say this. The Bible says man looks at the outward appearance, but it is God that looks at the heart. It would be great if people related to you only on the basis of who you are rather than how you look, but the truth is a good image in the first instance will arouse curiosity about the person behind the image.

Picture a person driving up to your house in a derelict car, which is coughing up smoke, and polluting the environment no end. He walks up to your door wearing a tight shiny suit, a crooked collar on his off white shirt, and what looks like a curry stain on his lapel. His shoes look like they haven't seen polish in months. But when he knocks on the door he announces that he is a financial advisor and he's been given your name by one of your friends and would like to recommend an investment vehicle to you. What are the chances you will buy what he has to offer? The way you dress really is the way you will be addressed.

How you look will also have a great impact on how you feel about yourself. Remember how you used to be when your mum bought you a new set of school uniform. You strutted your stuff all through the school day, even though everyone else was dressed just as smart as you were, but you didn't care. When you got home, you would carefully hang up your clothes so that they would be ready for the following day. Clothes do impact how you feel, and interestingly how you behave. If you are wearing a smart suit, you are less likely to engage in bullish behaviour, and more likely to be more composed in both manner and language. Who said clothes were not important?

Also when a man looks after himself people assume that he is likely to be responsible, particularly in business relationships, and they are more likely to trust him. Good grooming requires setting good habits in much the same way that living a healthy lifestyle will require the setting of good health habits. Many women find it difficult to tell their men that they have problems with how their men's breath or body smells, and because it is a hugely sensitive area, they suffer in silence. Body odour is not butch but highly offensive.

God is concerned with your physical well being. You must be too.

> *'Beloved I wish above all things that thou mayest prosper and*
> *be in health even as thy soul prospereth.'* **(3 John 2)**

Lesson 14 – A man and his God

Remember the former things, those of long ago;

I am God, and there is no other;

I am God, and there is none like me

I made known the end from the beginning,

From ancient times, what is still to come.

I say: My purpose will stand,

And I will do all that I please

From the east I summon a bird of prey;

From a far-off land, a man to fulfill my purpose

What I have said, that will I bring about

What I have planned, that I will do.

(Isaiah 46:9-11)

There are few more emotive topics than a discussion that centres on God. The debate will range from a heated argument about whether He actually exists, to a soporific outburst as to how He is responsible for every modern day calamity known to man. Somehow it is impossible for the majority to engage in a conversation about God without giving free rein to the multiplicity of emotions that a mention of His name evokes.

And yet when you really look at it, most of this negative emotion is horribly misdirected. Many can't (or choose not to) get their heads around the very real difference between God and religion. I learnt a definition many years ago that has held me in good stead and forever banished any confusion I had about why the distinction was so important. The word religion is derived from the Latin word '*religari*' which means 'to bind'. And in essence that's all religion does. It draws up a long list of rules, regulations and laws that must be adhered to if one is subscribe to God's standards of righteousness. It is man's desperate and ultimately doomed attempt, to draw closer to God by fulfilling an ever swelling catalogue of does and don'ts. It would be almost comical if it wasn't for the sometimes tragic consequences of these attempts. So now what happens is everyone runs around furiously doing their best to be good and frowning disapprovingly on anyone who violates even the smallest part of the rules. So now, only men can wear trousers, the use of makeup is strongly discouraged, and prayers have to be said in a preapproved posture.

And many of the people involved in these practices are genuine and well meaning. They have a genuine desire to please God and to live lives that are disciplined and honourable. But if history has taught us anything, it is that even the vilest of practices – racism, murders, rapes, lynchings and terrorist bombings, can be carried out and defended in a misguided use of God's name. And what starts out as genuine zeal can quickly become dark and evil.

Another equally disturbing offshoot of this kind of thinking is the belief that in order to become more acceptable to God, one must subject himself to various forms of physical and emotional pain. So every year we see converts hanging themselves on crosses, piercing their organs in macabre ceremonies and starving themselves to the point of death. The reasoning is that God will see their efforts and reward them accordingly.

It is not at all surprising that men of all ages, colours and ethnic backgrounds desperately seek after God in all of these different ways. After all, there is in every human being an innate longing and hunger for something bigger than himself. An awareness that, despite the many schools of thought that exist to the contrary, an Intelligent Designer does exist, responsible not only for the creation of the world, but also involved in the loving design of each individual with their peculiar quirks and shortcomings, and yet remarkable individuality and value. What is perturbing however is the fact that in spite of every effort made by God to reveal Himself to men, many still choose to relate to him on the basis of presumption and inane tradition.

> '*And he said to them: "You have a fine way of setting aside the commands of God in order to observe your own traditions."*' (**Mark 7:9**)

From Genesis to Revelation, God has engaged in the greatest act of self disclosure that the world will ever know, showing us who He really is, and not the ogre that religion has painted Him to be.

The truth is, the God that you see is the God that you will receive from. If you believe that God is a fierce enforcer of all that is morally and rigidly right, waiting to pounce on your every mistake, then inevitably your expectation will be that you ought to be punished for any slight deviation. Conversely if you believe that God is the purest example of a father, then you will understand the true nature of God. On the one hand His undying love and commitment to you. On the other, His firm discipline, which is the hallmark of any good father. In the increasingly liberal times we live in, love has come to be defined as allowing people to define for themselves what is good and what is wrong. But God has shown us what love really is, and in the same breath shown us the essence of He truly is.

'For God so greatly loved and dearly prized the world that He even gave up His only begotten, unique Son, so that whoever believes in, trusts in clings to, relies on Him shall not perish, (come to destruction, be lost) but have eternal (everlasting) life. For God did not send the Son into the world in order to judge (to reject, to condemn, to pass sentence on the world, but that the world might find salvation and might be made safe and sound through Him'. **(John 3:16-17)**

This is what distinguishes the God of the Bible from every other god. Because instead of wanting to be identified by His majesty, His omnipresence, His awesome creative ability, God elects to be known as a God of love who desires only the very best for those who are His.

"Or what man is there of you, if his son asks him for a loaf of bread will hand him a stone? Or if he asks for a fish, will hand him a serpent? If you then, evil as you are, know how to give good and advantageous gifts to your children, how much more will your Father who is in heaven, perfect as He is, give good and advantageous things to those that ask Him? **(Matthew 7: 9-11)**

Every man will at one time or another come face to face with who he really is. He will discover that despite his best efforts at goodness, it is so easy for him to move from angelic behaviour to that which can only be described as devilish in nature. He will come to the end of himself and be faced with situations that He simply cannot solve himself. He will encounter conundrums that defy human logic and ability. And when he finally accepts his limitations and expresses his need for help, he will find that the loving arms of God were extended to him the whole time.

So religion will never cut it. It was never meant to. Instead, right from the very beginning it was God's intention to create man so that he could have a relationship with Him. He wanted to work with him in partnership. And even after the sad debacle of Adam's treacherous sale of his birthright, God never gave up on man but continued to devise ways to restore that broken fellowship

Attacks on God unfailingly include unbridled attacks on the veracity of His word. How many times have you heard someone ask the question 'Who wrote the Bible? This is an unabashed attack on the integrity of God's Word. But the Bible answers this valid question very simply:

'All scripture is inspired by God and is useful to teach us what is true and to make us realize what is wrong in our lives. It corrects us when we are wrong and teaches us to do what is right.' **(2 Timothy 3:16)**

The best way I know how to explain this is using a simple analogy. When I was 15 years old, I laid eyes for the first time on the woman who would eventually become my wife and the mother of my children. I was smitten immediately and promised that I would do whatever it took to spend the rest of my life with this beautiful angel. Being a budding Romeo, I went home and began to pen a wonderful ode to the woman of my dreams. I got a chance a few days later to read this poem to her and she loved it. But here's my point. I *wrote* the poem, but without the inspiration that wifey gave me, that poem would never have been written. Similarly men were the instruments used to communicate God's will to us in writing, but without His inspiration, none of it would have ever been written.

I can genuinely understand why some men are put off by the idea of developing a relationship with God. After all as His representatives on the earth, we don't always portray Him in the best light. Much of what is put forward as doctrine is often only our own limited experience couched in language that makes it sound spiritual. Or often because we haven't taken the time to really study for ourselves what the Word of God says, we make it up as we go along and confuse ourselves and others in the process.

Many never admit it when they themselves miss the mark, but walk about instead with an air of superiority that makes everyone else feel as if they are destined for hell and weren't even worth dying for. People are obviously put off by such showiness, and it does nothing to truly represent the One we say we serve. Jesus clearly had a huge problem with this kind of behaviour as evidenced by his frequent railing against the Pharisees who were truly proficient in this kind of behaviour.

> *"Woe to you, teachers of the law and Pharisees, you hypocrites! You give a tenth of your spices – mint, dill and cumin. But you have neglected the more important matters of the law – justice, mercy and faithfulness. You should have practiced the latter, without neglecting the former."* **(Matthew 23:23)**

Do I understand everything about God. Of course not. But I know enough to know that God is real. That He has my best interests at heart. That when I miss the mark, I can call upon His mercy. That when I am clueless about which direction to take, I can call upon His counsel. That when I am overwhelmed by the pressures of life and want to give up on my marriage, my business, my life, I can lean on Him for indescribable strength.

Some people have made it a life vocation to study God. To try and compartmentalise Him and reduce Him to a list of principles. Admittedly there are laws that govern how God operates. But to limit Him in this way is to deny yourself the pleasure of discovering and enjoying fellowship with a living God who is far bigger than just a bunch of theological principles. So it is possible to spend years building an impressive resume of qualifications and still have absolutely no real life experience of the God you profess to have studied so much. That's not too different from spending a decade studying all of the principles that govern how to have a great marriage but never actually getting married and thus being able to put them into practice.

> *'Who also hath made us able ministers of the new testament; not of the letter, but of the spirit: for the letter killeth but the spirit giveth life.'* **(2 Corinthians 3:6)**

When I was younger, and didn't know better, I blamed God for everything that went wrong in my life. My reasoning was quite simple. Because God was all powerful and in control of everything, presumably if anything went wrong it was His fault. But as I grew older and became a father in my own right I began to truly understand the true complexities of fatherhood. Blamed for things that are not your fault. Expected to have the solution to every problem. Never considered by your children, because to them their needs only are paramount. Children are selfish and as I marvelled at this realization, I came to see how selfish and inconsiderate I had been in my walk with God.

I have never been big on trying to scare people into a relationship with God, because I don't really see the point. When I was a teenager, I distinctly remember a self-styled end time prophet who used to stand at a prominent street corner and bellow out daily warnings about God's imminent judgement and the fire and brimstone that awaited those who didn't turn from their wicked ways. I also remember the fear that would grip me whenever I would hear him on any of my forays into town. I am pretty sure that there must have been some who were scared into changing their ways but I doubt that there were any whose love for God was enhanced as a result.

> *'Or despisest thee the riches of His goodness and forbearance and longsuffering; not knowing that the goodness of God leadeth thee to repentance?'* **(Romans 2:4)**

It goes without saying that impending judgement is real and that people must be warned about the reality of hell but this if often done without highlighting all of God's efforts to ensure that none of His children go to hell unless they actively choose to. People won't go to hell because they are wicked, or have messed up in so many ways. They will go to hell because they reject Jesus and it is this message that needs to be preached from the mountain tops.

As God's ambassadors, it is our responsibility to portray him and His message correctly. An ambassador never speaks on his own authority but is tasked with communicating the statements of those whom he represents. Can you imagine the ambassador of a country speaking to the media in the country he has been posted to and telling them words to this effect: 'My President has an opinion on this matter that I don't agree with'. That ambassador would be recalled immediately and relieved of his diplomatic duties. God trusts us to represent him, but if we fail to do so, we revoke His mandate by our arrogance.

> *"For I have not spoken of myself, but the Father which sent me, he gave me a commandment, what I should say and what I should speak. And I know that his commandment is life everlasting: whatsoever I speak therefore, even as the Father said unto me, so I speak."* **(John 12:49-50)**

The most exciting thing about developing a relationship with God is that it is the only place in the world where you will discover true fulfilment. A great marriage, a wonderful job, stacks of cash are all good things. But as good as they are, they can only complement who God is and are not a substitute for His role in your life. Take the time to discover Him for yourself. It will be the best thing you will ever do.

Lesson 15 – A man and his woman

Men commit over 90 percent of major crimes of violence, 100 percent of the rapes, 95 percent of the burglaries. They comprise 94 percent of our drunken drivers, 70 percent of suicides, 91 percent of offences against family and children. Single men comprise between 80 and 90 percent of most of the categories of social pathology, and on the average they make less money than any other group in the society – yes, less than single women or working women. As any insurance actuary will tell you, single men are also less responsible about their bills, their driving and other personal conduct. Together with the disintegration of the family, they constitute our leading social problem. **George Gilder – Sexual Suicide, The New York Times Book Co.**

I don't think there has been a time in all of human history, that the sexuality of men has been rehashed and redefined more than in our present day. Our generation has gone all out to move all the goalposts and signposts that commonly pointed men to acceptable sexual behaviour. What was considered honourable and traditional is now ridiculed, and this disdain has caused genuine confusion for most men. They are no longer sure how to relate to women. Chivalry is out, and a frantic desire to copulate with anything with a pulse has taken its place. And although modern societal norms tend to trivialize any mention of these issues, they have far reaching implications for male life in this generation and beyond.

Contrary to the images we are bombarded with by the media of alternative family structures, studies have shown that the traditional unit of husband and wife in a marriage relationship remains the basis on which enduring societies are built. Dr. Charles Winick at City University of New York studied more than two thousand of the cultures that have existed in the history of the world. He found only fifty five where the lines between masculinity and femininity were blurred. And not one of these societies survived for more than a few years. We may think that as we have become more and more technologically savvy we can ignore our Judaeo-Christian values with impunity. But history paints an entirely different picture.

There was a time when the roles that men and women played were so clearly defined that there really was no issue to discuss. The woman stayed at home and was responsible for looking after the house and the children and all the attendant duties that went with these functions. The fact that she had a womb and was physically suited to child bearing made it patently clear how society would be structured. The man on the other hand would go out and bear the brunt of providing for his family. He had a job that kept him away from the family home, sometimes for months on end. He would ensure that the physical needs of his family were met. He did not always meet the emotional needs of his wife or children, but that's how it was. And everybody accepted it.

But times are a changing. Because of the increased and welcome acceptance of women as equal partners in society, the pressures of providing for a family on a single income, and many other varying factors, the dynamics of the male and female relationship have changed forever. The term 'housewife' has become a misnomer, a symbol of female oppression and inferiority. Women have taken up dominant positions in industry and in government whilst at the other end of the spectrum, men have begun to replace their customary role in the workplace with permanent roles in the home. Everything has changed irrevocably.

The legislature and the judiciary had a huge part to play in this metamorphosis. Laws were passed and interpreted that made it clear that inequality of the sexes was no longer to be tolerated. And the huge strides forward that societies have made in the last fifty years are in many ways testament to the real benefits of genuinely embracing the input of the fifty percent of the population that had been largely ignored until recently.

But as with many positive developments, there was a real and very sinister dark side. Feminist ideology swept through the nations, leaving a trail of division and militancy in its wake. Suddenly, there was a class of women who had gone from being largely ignored or tolerated, to themselves replicating many of the male excesses they had despised so much. They were cavalier in their sexuality, no longer yearning for permanency in relationships, but content to also move seamlessly from one relationship to another. Women had always been the defenders, if not the enforcers of virtue, but not any more.

As a result of all these developments, both positive and negative, men were no longer sure how to relate to women. They had to deal with women who were more confident, often earned more money than they did, and generally were unwilling to put up with chauvinism in all its forms. They would no longer put up with physical abuse or rape. They demanded equal opportunity and were good value for it. No longer were women to be viewed merely as notches on a belt, as prey for sexual predators. Now the levels of accountability required of men had risen considerably and rightly so.

I despise men who have no concept of the real role that they were created to play. Men who do not understand that their unbridled sexual aggression and accompanying immaturity is largely responsible for the broken homes and single parent families that are such a problem today. Contrary to popular opinion, manhood will never be defined by the number of women you sleep with or the number of children you sire. The standards are much more stringent.

Oh how the beauty of God's original plan has been perverted! The first man was given a woman who he was to provide for, protect, and share his life and authority with. He would focus his passion on his wife and their sexual union would result in mutual pleasure and ultimately in offspring that would replicate the beauty of their parents' relationship. A stable society and civilisation would result from the widespread growth of millions of such relationships. I quote at length from the good book:

> *"Drink waters out of your own cistern, of a pure marriage relationship, and fresh running waters out of your own well. Should your offspring be dispersed abroad as water brooks in the streets? Confine yourself to your own wife; let your children be for you alone, and not the children of strangers with you. Let your fountain of human life be blessed with the rewards of fidelity and rejoice in the wife of your youth. Let her be as the loving hind and pleasant doe, tender, gentle, attractive – let her bosom satisfy you at all times, and always be transported with delight in her love. Why should you my son be infatuated with a loose woman, embrace the bosom of an outsider and go astray?*

> *For the ways of man are directly before the eyes of the Lord and he who would have us live soberly, chastely and godly, carefully weighs all man's goings. His own iniquities shall ensnare the wicked man, and he shall be held with the cords of his sin. He will die for lack of discipline and instruction, and in the greatness of his folly he will go astray and be lost."* **(Proverbs 5:15-23)**

Instead, sexual experimentation, promiscuity, and a preponderance of sexual disease have resulted. The media waxes lyrical of the pleasure that fornication and adultery will bring, but neglects to mention the heartbreak, the emotional confusion and untimely deaths that accompany such 'pleasure'. They will encourage you to masturbate, but not tell you that this act on its own will bring with it lifelong feelings of self-condemnation, separation from God and an inability to be satisfied with whichever woman you find. Social engineers will tell you that the only person who can truly understand a man is another man, and so encourage homosexual relationships which are anathema to a productive society. Pornography, bestiality, incest, necrophilia are all expressions of those who professing to be wise, become fools. Nay, friends, in the beginning it was not so.

> *"Husbands, love your wives even as Christ loved the Church and gave Himself for it."* **(Ephesians 5:25)**

The command itself may be brief, but it comes with great responsibility. When he asks a woman for her hand in marriage, a man is saying by this act that his heart has chosen her among all women and that he loves her more than any other. At the altar he pledges to continue that love until death parts them. And even after her youthful beauty has begun to fade, and the sparkle has left her eyes, even as old age brings with it menopause and then wrinkles, the faithful husband's love remains as deep as ever. His heart is still to find its truest delight in her.

Every man has to realize that when his woman places her life in his hands and agrees to become his wife, she has entrusted him with not just her life, but with everything that comes with it. Her hopes and fears, joys and sorrows, her shortcomings and her vulnerability. This requires the man to learn the art of gentleness. He may be faithful and true to her, but lack that affection in speech and action that has the power to truly satisfy her heart. And the trouble with many men is that they often fall into free and careless habits at home, which they wouldn't even dream of displaying in public. They will pride themselves on their thoughtfulness and sensitivity, but at home too often they are rude, careless in speech, and don't pay enough attention to their words and actions. They forget that their wives can be easily hurt. Often a man thinks that just because a woman is his woman, she should know he loves her even when he is rude to her, and that she should endure anything he says or does, even if it is something that would sorely hurt or offend any other woman.

Because she is his woman, he actually owes her the greatest respect. There should be no other woman whose feelings he should be so careful about or whom he should so grieve to hurt. Sadly, there are many men who would never speak badly to their wives but few if any tender words ever fall from their lips. They have forgotten the warmth of the newly wed husband and their speech to their wives has become cold and businesslike. Silence is obviously better than angry words, just like a barren garden is better than a patch of weeds. But a garden full of beautiful flowers is better still.

There are also other times that require thoughtfulness by the man. Sometimes she is very tired. She may have had a particularly trying day at work or at home. A sick child, an irate boss, a broken relationship. What is her man to do in these instances? This is his opportunity to demonstrate his love for her, to impart strength and peace. Every wife wants to know that her husband understands her, will protect her, and is willing to sacrifice his own comfort to ensure hers. Self has to die. His primary goal is to bring pleasure to her. No sacrifice is too great. What Jesus Christ is to us as His children, every husband is to his woman in his own unique way.

He must honour his wife, in the same way that he did before she became his wife. He opened doors for her, lay awake at night thinking about her. To him she epitomised beauty and nobility. When she becomes his wife should he honour her any less? Marriage is the second greatest covenant on earth, second only to the awesome covenant of salvation between man and God. The man links his life with his wife's and whatever affects one now affects the other. He honours her by generously providing for her to the best of his ability. He honours her by knowing her intimately. He honours her by sharing his life with her. By seeking her counsel and not treating her as a child. He honours her by not betraying her trust and commitment and sharing his bed and his heart with any other woman.

Do you know how many men routinely treat their wives as second class citizens and never solicit their opinions on matters that will affect their livelihood? She may not be qualified to professionally advise him on his business ventures, but she loves him and the importance of that cannot be overemphasised. Her cheerful encouragement and warm sympathy when things don't go right are indispensable, just as her gleeful delight at your successes will warm your heart.

And often it is the fact that a man loves his wife so much that causes him to keep things from her that he feels may cause her distress and anxiety. Such a course is both wrong and unwise. Whatever concerns him concerns her also. He has no interests which are not hers as well as his. She should share all of his life. She should know of all his successes and triumphs and be allowed to rejoice with him in his gladness. If trials come, she should know also of these, so that she may sympathize with him and encourage him in his struggles. 'For better or worse' is not just a cute phrase that people recite at the altar for the wedding guests to hear. Her counsel and intuitive awareness often proves to be of more value than the advice of even the shrewdest businessmen. Many men would have been greater, or not failed so often if they had genuinely consulted their wives instead of only coming to her with *a fait accompli*.

Every husband should honour his wife by proving himself worthy of her. The love of a good woman has lifted even the lowliest of men to lofty positions in society. Spurred on by her ardent affection, he has realized supposedly impossible ambition. Every husband should do everything within his power to be worthy of the wife he has already won. He should improve his character at every opportunity and eliminate every bad habit. For her sake as well as his own he should reach out and achieve everything he was created to achieve. Every possibility in his soul should be developed. He should never be a tyrant, playing the petty despot in his home. A true man demonstrates his character everywhere, but nowhere moreso than in his own home. He has the power in his hands to create the atmosphere in which his wife will blossom. A husband who is generous within his own doors will not be close and stingy outside. He has an awesome opportunity to practice every virtue under the watchful eye of those who love him the most. Then when the time comes to display those virtues in a public forum, he will not be found wanting.

And finally, but most importantly, every husband should walk with and instruct his wife in her walk with God. Many good men love their wives and sacrifice for them at the drop of a hat. They bless them with tenderness and affection. They honour them and succeed in bringing many noble achievements to lay at their wives feet. They share every burden and walk close beside them in every trial. But when it comes to a personal relationship with Her Creator, the husbands are content to draw back and let their wives go it alone. While the wife goes to church with the kids, the husband waits outside, or worse still stays at home. At the very point where his interest in her life should be the deepest it fails altogether. So she has to carry the responsibility for the children's' spiritual instruction all alone, and bow her head alone in prayer to God.

A man's love for his wife should push him to desire to enjoy the beauty of corporate fellowship with his wife. It will strengthen their marriage and unite their hearts, since it is only those who realize the full sweetness of wedded life who are one in purpose and hope, and whose souls are knitted together. Why should a man and a woman spend years on earth in growing into one, only to be separated by the eternal chasm between heaven and hell?

A good woman will bring out every latent gifting that a man has buried deep within him. She will motivate him to become better than he could become without her inspiration. He too must do everything within his power to make her life and her value appreciate. For her to depreciate on his watch is truly reprehensible.

Lesson 16 - A man and his motives

"And you my son Solomon, acknowledge the God of your father, and serve him with wholehearted devotion and with a willing mind, for the Lord searches every heart and understands every motive behind the thoughts. If you seek him, he will be found by you; but if you forsake him, he will reject you forever." **(1 Chronicles 28:9)**

People very rarely act without a motive. They are motivated by so many different things. Profit, advantage, reward, greed, love, hate, envy or jealousy. And really when you look at it, a positive or negative motive is often the only difference between doing something that is of genuine benefit to others and accomplishing something that only raises your own stock and profile.

Much good can result when one has a pure motive. Good that will not only help others, but yourself also. A pure and strong motive gives you staying power in the face of adversity. It also says a lot about your character, and demonstrates your sincerity like very few other things can.

But on the other side of the scale, we have what has commonly come to be known as the 'ulterior motive'. That human object or aim that goes beyond what one professes with their lips. It never considers the interests of others and is at all times self seeking and utterly selfish.

All of us do things because we are motivated by personal advantage. When I was in high school I used to faithfully leave the halls of residence every Sunday morning and make my way down to the cathedral in the City for morning mass. To all and sundry I looked like a young man who had nothing but God on his mind and I know there were some people who saw me in my smart school blazer and slacks who thought of me as an example of youthful Christian zeal. But how wrong they were! The bottom line is I went to church because it was the only way of getting away from the dull routine of boarding school life that did not involve legging it over the wall when no one was watching. Secondly, and more importantly, I got the chance to do a spot of 'bird' watching – drooling over the girls from the local convent who also attended the same church service! My Church attendance was a good thing, but my motive for doing it was never the right one.

In business circles, the phrase 'There is no such thing as a free lunch' is in common use. It simply means that if someone other than a friend takes you to lunch they usually have a business motive for doing so. They want something from you, and don't simply have a sincere interest in your dietary well-being. And in personal relationships, who can fail to identify with the wife who turns around and suspiciously asks her husband, 'Why are you being so nice to me all of a sudden?' Or point out the man who offers to serve his Pastor in one capacity or another, not so much because he particularly wants to serve him, but because he sees an opportunity to gain recognition and influence for himself.

Whenever we do things, we must have a clear understanding of why we do them. Everyone may think we are great because we do wonderful things for others, but deep down we may know that our real reason for doing those things was because there was something in it for us. And I am not for a moment suggesting that we all suddenly begin putting everyone's interests above our own. Even the Bible tells you to love your neighbour as yourself. I am addressing here the cold and calculating motive with which many of us establish relationships with others or serve them. Delilah pleaded with Samson to tell her the secret of his strength not because she truly wanted to get to know him, but because she had been paid by the Philistine lords to betray him.

'And she said to him, "How can you say, I love you, when your heart is not with me? You have mocked me these three times and have not told me in what your great strength lies". And when she pressed him day after day with her words and urged him, he was vexed to death. Then he told her all his mind and said to her, "A razor has never come upon my head, for I have been a Nazirite to God from my birth. If I am shaved, then my strength will go from me, and I shall become weak and be like any other man."

And when Delilah saw that he had told her all his mind, she went and called for the Philistine lords. Saying, "Come up this once, for he has told me all he knows". Then the Philistine lords came up to her and brought the money in their hands.' **(Judges 16:15-18)**

And what is really interesting about motives is that unless we have a keen sense of self awareness, we can get to the stage where we convince ourselves that our selfish motives are actually good. If you tell yourself a lie long enough, you will eventually begin to believe it. And when our own motives are suspicious or untoward, we tend to become suspicious of the motives and actions of others. And even when they are genuine and well intentioned, our negative wiring makes us see others the way we are.

It is a fundamental law of life that whatever you are willing to make happen for others, God will make happen for you. The truth is, we don't really believe that, otherwise you would see a marked change in the way we relate to other people and their needs.

'And if you have not proved faithful in that which belongs to another, whether God or man, who will give you that which is your own? **(Luke 16:12)**

When we are motivated only by personal gain, the only question we ever ask is, 'What's in it for me?' And the inevitable results are friction, tension, competitive jealousy and frustration. When you start a business for example your primary motive must be the provision of a quality service to as many people as possible. In doing this, you will make more money than you ever imagined possible. Most men start a business however with the express aim of making as much money as possible, regardless of the personal cost. So they cheat, lie, steal, and defraud their customers, and often seem to get away with it. But the Bible has a chilling edict for them:

'A faithful man shall abound with blessings, but he who makes haste to be rich at any cost shall not go unpunished'. **(Proverbs 28:20)**

The wrong motive can result in consequences more dire than we could have ever imagined. Just ask Ananias and Sapphira. Their story is proof of the fact that what can start out as an apparently innocent desire for public recognition and feting can easily turn into a disaster. If you don't know the story, here it is in brief.

In a Holy Ghost inspired show of Christian unity and comradeship, believers in the Book of Acts were selling their possessions and bringing the money to the apostles' feet for them to distribute and cater for the needs of all the other believers. Ananias and his wife Sapphira decided to get involved in the show and so they sold a piece of their property. I can just imagine Sapphira saying to her husband, "Now Ananias, you remember that at last week's meeting Levi and Rachel sold their plot of land and gave the money to Peter. Remember how everyone was so impressed with their generous gesture? We can't be outdone by them, so this week it's out turn. You'll need to make sure you buy me a new dress so that I look really good when we give the money".

But instead of taking all the money to the apostles, Ananias with his wife's knowledge and connivance wrongfully appropriated some of the proceeds and brought only a part to Peter. Peter's words to him are particularly insightful:

'But Peter said, "Ananias, why has Satan filled your heart that you should lie to and attempt to deceive the Holy Spirit, and should in violation of your promise withdraw secretly and appropriate to your own use part of the price from the sale of the land? As long as it remained unsold, was it not still your own? And even after it was sold was not the money at your disposal and under your control? Why then, is it that you have proposed and purposed in your heart to do this thing?...You have not simply lied to men, playing false and showing yourself utterly deceitful, but to God". Upon hearing these words, Ananias fell down and died. And great dread and terror took possession of all who heard of it'. **(Acts 5:3-5)**

Sapphira followed suit shortly afterwards. I wonder what would happen in our churches, on our jobs, and in our relationships if our motives were exposed in such a public manner. Jesus consistently took a similar swipe at the Pharisees who engaged in practices that were in themselves good Godly practices, but only did them so that people would applaud their humility and piety.

"Take care not to do your good deeds publicly or before men, in order to be seen by them; otherwise you will have no reward with and from your Father who is in heaven. Thus whenever you give to the poor, do not blow a trumpet before you, as the hypocrites in the synagogues and in the streets like to do, that they may be recognized and honoured and praised by men. Truly, I tell you, they have their reward in full already'.

Also when you pray, you must not be like the hypocrites, for they love to pray standing in the synagogues and on the corners of the streets, that they may be seen by people. Truly I tell you they have their reward in full already." **(Matthew 6:1-3,5)**

What is your motive for doing the things you do? To get a pat on the back? To get something for nothing? For those who will immediately decide that they will not do anything at all for fear of appearing to be courting publicity and fame, I bring this word of balance:

'Don't cherish exaggerated ideas of yourself or your importance, but try to have a sane estimate of your capabilities by the light of faith that God has given to you all...Through the grace of God we have different gifts. If our gift is preaching, let us preach to the limit of our vision. If it is serving others, let us concentrate on our service; if it is teaching let us give all we have to our teaching; and if our gift be the stimulating of the faith of others let us set ourselves to it. Let the man who is called to give give freely; let the man who wields authority think of his responsibilities; and let the man who feels sympathy for his fellows act cheerfully'. **(Romans 12:3-8)**

We are not to shun visibility, but we are to have pure motives in doing what we do. That way God gets the glory for the good that you do, you have an opportunity to live a full life, expressing the gifts that He has given you, and others get the benefit of enjoying the fruit of your wonderful skill and ability. Everybody wins.

And yet more often than not this warning will go unheeded. Men will continue to join churches so that they can build up their business contacts. They will continue to court women, and pimp themselves out so that they can take advantage of 'her daddy's money'. They will persist in being utterly ruthless and calculating, not realizing that in the final analysis, every impure motive will be exposed. Beware of those that say one thing with their lips, but their heart is not with you. Many a men has fallen prey to the wrong woman, or to the wrong business associate, because they didn't take the time to carefully consider the motives that the other party had.

"Never once did we try to win you with flattery, as you very well know." **(1 Thessalonians 2:5)**

The tragedy is that sometimes even with innocent and genuine motives, one can do themselves irreparable harm. Every motive has got to be tempered with wisdom and an acute understanding of the prevailing environment and people you are dealing with. Contrary to what you may want to believe, and despite your best efforts, there will always be people you come across who will seek only your harm, and in dealing with such be advised to exercise extreme caution.

'The thief comes only in order to steal and kill and destroy..' **(John 10:10)**

And for proof that even an innocent motive can get your fingers burnt, just ask Uzza.

'And when they came to the threshing floor of Chidon, Uzza put out his hand to steady the ark, for the oxen that were drawing the cart stumbled and were restive. And the anger of the Lord was kindled against Uzza, and He smote him because he touched the ark; and there he died before God.' **(1 Chronicles 13:9-10)**

One of the primary lessons that I have learnt from life is that when you do what is right, because it is right, a reward is inevitable. Because evil in not quickly punished, and good not immediately rewarded, there can often set in a despondency that convinces you that despite you trying to live right and do what is right, you are lagging behind those who do wrong and seemingly get away with it. But Galatians 6:7 tells you clearly:

"Do not be deceived and deluded and misled; God will not allow Himself to be sneered at, scorned, disdained or mocked by mere pretensions or professions, or by His precepts being set aside. He inevitably deludes himself who attempts to delude God. For whatever a man sows, that and that only is what he will reap".

Before I finish this lesson I want to quickly share with you three stories from the Word that will hopefully mark your conscience forever and convince you that good always wins out over evil, and that having the right motives and executing them effectively will always bring you out on top.

The first story is about a rich businessman by the name of Nabal who had a wife who was both wise and beautiful. Her name was Abigail. David and his men, who were on the run from Saul, sent word to Nabal asking him to provide food for them as they had not done any harm to his workers. But Nabal sneered at David's request and sent his messengers scurrying. When David got wind of this affront, he gathered his troops to go down to Maon and teach Nabal a lesson. But Abigail found out about it also, and immediately summoned her servants and prepared a great feast for David and his men. She pleaded with David to relent on his promise to wipe out Nabal and his family. David accepted what she had brought and commended her for her discretion and advice, agreeing not to destroy her family. Nabal meanwhile was drinking away merrily and became very drunk. The following morning however when Abigail told him what had happened, he collapsed with fear, and became paralyzed and helpless, dying a few days later. Not only did Abigail's wisdom save her family. Later she became David's wife and is often held up as an icon of female virtue and wisdom. Motivated by the need to protect her family, she ended up in a position of even greater wealth and influence. Nabal on the other hand, for all his wealth and influence only bears mention as an example of how impertinence and mockery can result in your untimely demise. He was motivated by pride and selfishness and he paid for these with his life.

The second story is told in the book of Esther of a man by the name of Haman, who I am inclined to believe was a close relative of Nabal whom we have just heard about, if not by blood then certainly by mindset. Very self seeking, and conniving, he was promoted by King Ahasuerus above all the other princes in the kingdom, and pride immediately set in. Shortly afterwards, he developed a grudge against Mordecai, Queen Esther's uncle because he refused to bow down to him. And instead of enjoying his new position and all its trappings, his blinding rage resulted in him plotting not only to get rid of Mordecai, but of all of the Jews, because he had discovered that Mordecai was Jewish. But as with so many evil motives, Haman's evil only resulted in his sworn enemy subsequently being feted by the king, him being hung on the gallows he had erected for Mordecai and the evil decree that had been made against the Jews being revoked.

But the tale that warms my heart more than any other is that of the Shunamite woman. She was a rich and influential woman. Every time the prophet Elisha would pass by her area she would plead with him to spend some time with them, and prepare a meal for him. Recognizing that Elisha was a true man of God, she spoke with her husband, and convinced him to prepare a chamber for the man of God so that whenever he passed by he would have a place to stay. This selfless act resulted not only in God blessing her with a child as she had been unable to have any children, but in that same child being brought back from the dead when he had died unexpectedly.

And nowhere is an honest examination of our motives more important than in our walk with God. Sometimes we can be doing a great job in serving Him, but lose sight of why we are doing it, and get caught up in the hype of it all. Our character is always going to be more important than our reputation. We owe it to ourselves to remember why we are in this race in the first place.

> *"You have endured hard times because of me and you have not given up. But I do have something against you. And it is this: You don't have as much love as you used to. Think where you have fallen from, and then turn back and do as you did at first."* **(Revelation 2:3-5)**

Lesson 17 - A man and his legacy

What Will You Leave Behind?

Your footprints in this world will not stay

Just like footprints in the snow they will fade away

One day you will be a memory to the people you leave behind

Will remembering you bring gladness

or will you be forgotten over the course of time?

Will you leave behind a beauty that can not be seen with eyes

But will remain forever because it never dies

Will you leave words of comfort to others while you sleep

As they have the peace of knowing where you are

Even tho' they weep

Will the seeds you have sown along life's way

be worthy of harvest on God's Judgement Day

Will you be welcomed into Heaven because your name

is found written in God's Precious Book

Or will you be turned away as Jesus gives you His last Loving look

The way you will be remembered is completely up to you

Because the choices that you make in this life

82

and the things that you do

Will all be deciding factors on what you leave behind

So what will be your legacy when you face the end of time?

Janice Stancil

> *And in the end it's not the years in your life that count. It's
> the life in your years.* **Abraham Lincoln**

> *Don't measure yourself by what you have accomplished, but by what you
> should have accomplished with your ability.* **John Wooden**

Every man will one day find himself in the autumn of his life. That day comes at different times for each man. For some the autumn will come all too prematurely in their infancy, before they have had a chance to really live at all. For others, tragedy strikes and they are cut off in their prime. And for others still, it will come at an advanced age when the scenes of your youth have fled forever. Even now, when you take stock of your past you marvel at how age has caught you by surprise. And were it not for the aches and pains that accompany old age, and your altered image in the mirror, you would easily forget that you were indeed old.

Many of the friends you knew and counselled with are long gone. For some your spouses may have departed also. And although time may have healed the pain of your bereavement, there often remains a void in your heart that cannot be filled, and a sober awareness that you too are destined to follow in their footsteps.

But the bitterest of all reflections, regardless of when our time on this earth is up, is that of realizing that we have wasted our lives, and that we cannot go back and make good the years that we have misused. The awareness that regardless of how deep our desire may be to roll back the years and do things differently, there are some things that simply cannot be changed.

However I encourage you not to give in to despondency. Although you may have seen loved ones pass on, made some terrible mistakes in your life, and even lost fame and fortune, remember the enduring promises of God concerning you and be encouraged. He declared for all time that He would never leave you or forsake you. That regardless of what kind of predicament you ever found yourself in, He would be your way of escape. The prophet Habakkuk who triumphantly declared,

> *"Even though the fig trees have no fruit and no grapes grow on the vines, even
> though the olive crop fails and the fields produce no grain, even though the sheep
> all die and the cattle stalls are empty, I will still be joyful and glad, because the
> Lord God is my Saviour. The Sovereign Lord gives me strength. He makes me sure-
> footed as a deer and keeps me safe on the mountains."* **(Habakkuk 3:17-19)**

It is easy to give in to negativity. It is easier still to reflect forlornly on what could have been. Instead, realize that as long as you are alive, you still have an opportunity to do more, to become more, and to bless the lives of those around you.

"Do not forget to do good and to help one another, because these are the sacrifices that please God." **(Hebrews 13:16)**

As long as there is breath in your body, you still have a purpose to fulfil on the earth. The Bible tells you that it is better to be a living dog than a dead lion. It is a tragedy to see men as they grow old give up on their own dreams, and opt to live vicariously through their children. Do not give up on your studies, your business or your other pursuits. Keep your mind alert and active. Avoid becoming unduly dependant on others for your financial and physical upkeep. Your children and your loved ones will respect you more if they don't have to provide for your every need. Endeavour to be as useful as you can be whilst you are still here. And although your physical strength may have waned, you still have the advantage of a keen mind and the years of experience that you can make use of.

Often, as a result of advanced age one is no longer able to do what they were accustomed to doing before, and many times someone younger assumes their role. When this happens there is a tendency to feel as if the world is militating against you. It is easy to live in the past and believe that every innovation and advance taking place around you should be criticised. And it is easy to become more sensitive to things that you would have shrugged off before. Offences assume greater significance than they need to. Choose to forgive quickly and to be cheerful and affectionate with all.

I think it was Cicero in his Treatise on Old Age that said, when talking about the effects of old age on memory, that he had never heard of a miser forgetting the place where he had buried his treasure. What the mind prizes most, it retains. If you prize the beautiful memories of your past, you will remember them when you need them most, and they will sustain you when you are tempted to only remember the bad times.

What would God have you do? We are not privileged to be able to fold our hands and revel in idleness as if we have finished our course. Man was never made to be idle, and in all honesty will soon discover that his happiness is intimately connected with his labour. You may not be able to use your physical body as freely as you did before, but you can still use your tongue to praise your God. You can still use your tongue to instruct the young on the wisdom it has taken you a lifetime to accumulate. Old age often gives you the opportunity to say things that you may not have been able to get away with in your earlier years. Use that opportunity to speak a word in season and change someone's destiny.

But what is of paramount importance is the condition of your heart. The older man can serve God just as effectively as the younger man if his heart is right. God is so awesome! He recognises that all His children have a role to play in establishing His kingdom if they are truly committed to Him. While Joshua and the Israelites waged war against the Amalekites it was actually an ageing Moses who orchestrated their victory by lifting up his hands in prayer. When through fatigue he could no longer hold them up, the Amalekites prevailed, and it was only when Aaron and Hur assisted him that the battle was won. Both the young and the old have a part to play, in partnership, in fulfilling God's plan. If you cannot preach, you can, by prayer, hold up the hands of those who do. Even the birth of baby Jesus was preceded by the prayers of sages Anna and Simeon who never left the temple, but were instrumental in ushering in the One who would bring salvation to Israel.

Remember to always be thankful. In God's mercy you have been protected while many of your peers have been cut off in their prime. You may have enjoyed prosperity that others only dreamed of having. You may have had parents who nurtured you and gave you the best opportunities to make a success of your life. He gave you faithful friends, first grade teachers, excellent health and a sound mind. But the thing you need to be most grateful for is that He saved you from a path of iniquity and ignominy and adopted you into His family. He gave you an opportunity to be an instrument of good in the earth.

And now we come to the issue of your own departure from this earth. There may be many uncertain things in the earth, but this is not one of them. If a man does not meet Jesus in the clouds upon His return for His church, it is appointed for all men to die. But even the prospect of physical death no longer holds any fear for those of us who have accepted the gift of eternal life lovingly held out to us by a compassionate Saviour:

'O, death where is thy sting? O, grave where is thy victory.' **(1 Corinthians 15:55)**

Death, when viewed from a natural standpoint, is truly a fearful event. The final separation between the soul and body is usually accompanied by a convulsive struggle. It is made all the more scary by being separated permanently from everything that is familiar. But for those who die in the Lord, there is the promise of rest, a cessation of trouble and an eternity spent with God. Regardless of the excesses of your youth and the sin that may have characterised your life, it is not too late to change your final destination. Nowhere is there a more glaring example of the compassion of our Lord than in the conversion of one of the criminals at Calvary:

"But the other criminal protested, "Don't you fear God even when you have been sentenced to die? We deserve to die for our crimes, but this man hasn't done anything wrong." Then he said, "Jesus, remember me when you come into your Kingdom." And Jesus replied, "I assure you, today you will be with me in paradise." **(Luke 23:40-43)**

And yet the mercy of God saved even him. Nothing excludes you from salvation, unless you choose to reject the invitation freely held out to you. Death came into the world as a result of the sin of man, and consequently man became subject to his environment and also became aware that he would now return to the dust of the earth from where he had come. But those who are saved will never see death. Jesus Christ, the defender of all things pure and true, has purchased through His death and resurrection eternal life for all who are willing to put their trust in Him. Death in its previous form no longer exists for those who pass on in the Lord. They do not die, they sleep. The Bible tells us that when the apostle Stephen was being stoned by his false accusers, his life was not taken away from him, but he gave it up, in much the same way that Jesus did.

"And he kneeled down, and cried with a loud voice, "Lord, lay not this sin to their charge". And when he had said this, he fell asleep". **(Acts 7:60)**

For the children of God death has lost its sting. It has the outward appearance of death, but its nature has changed. That which used to be a curse is actually now a blessing.

"For all things are yours, whether Paul, or Apollos, or Cephas, or the world, or life, or death, or things present, or things to come, all are yours." **(1 Corinthians 3:22)**

On the other side of this coin are the many men who have experienced the woes and storms that are an inevitable part of life, and without acknowledging it to themselves or others, have thrown in the towel, and given up on life, longing only for the sweet rest that death promises. They are aware of the consequences of suicide, and so they wait impatiently for the day when the curtain comes down on their life as a result of age or some other welcome mishap. The only problem with this defeatist way of thinking is that it makes a mockery of your original purpose for being on this earth. It ignores the fact that each and every one of us has something we were created to accomplish, not just for our own benefit, but for the benefit of a designated segment of humanity. There is a group of people who will never achieve their destiny if you fail to achieve yours. They are waiting on you to release the seeds of greatness that are in you so that you may in turn motivate them to become all they were created to become.

And so as I talk about a man's legacy, do not confuse this with a man's profile. In this day, there are many who crave fame for fame's sake. They would gladly be well known for anything, rather than suffer the supposed stigma of being unknown. And so we have bred a class of people who will go to any ends to gain notoriety even if it means they have to sell their souls to achieve it. They will compromise their beliefs, betray those near and dear to them and lose their self respect in a desperate attempt to achieve significance.

No, when we talk about legacy, I am referring to what people will remember about you when you are long gone. Will they remember your acts of kindness, your generosity, your strength? Or will they recall your cynicism, your meanness and your fault finding?

Those who are truly great are often not fondly remembered when they are alive. In his lifetime, Martin Luther King Jnr. was vilified, despised and ultimately murdered. And yet today his message of reconciliation, his belief in the equality of all men and his passion for the cessation of a culture of hate and violence has inspired men of all colours to order their societies to exemplify these ideals.

You may be privileged to be acknowledged in your lifetime. But even if that never happens, that must not deter you from pursuing a course that you know is right. Your impact on this generation cannot be measured by how often you appear on television, how many times your face is on the cover of the glossiest magazines, or how many invitations you received to the grandest events on the social calendar. These things in themselves can often be an indicator of the impact that one is having. But you must realize that many of the most significant and influential people that this world has been privileged to know were never feted in their lifetime. And yet their names will go down in the annals of history for the impact they had on their generation.

It is a travesty to go through this life and have no one remember that you were ever here. There are books to be written, songs to be sung, opulent architectural structures to be designed. Each and every man must take it as his lifelong ambition to leave something of value for those who are to come after him. Everyone understands the value of leaving a financial inheritance for your family. But that should only be a part of a man's legacy. A man's character is what he will truly be remembered for. And a man's family will be his greatest inheritance.

'He who troubles his family will inherit the wind.' (**Proverbs 11:29**)

It is never too early to start thinking about the kind of impact you will have on your generation and those to come. In fact, the earlier a man begins to carefully consider his legacy, the better a man he will be during his lifetime. More often than not, people begin to consider the overall impact of their lives when they're just about to or have already retired. The truth is, you only have one bite of the cherry at life as we know it.

When one is looking ahead at how he wants his life to play out, success is high on his agenda. But when you are looking back, you will want to know that your efforts were seen and felt in a positive way by all the people they came into contact with.

There is such a thing as a negative legacy. For every positive and uplifting legacy, there is an equally negative and damaging one. Charles Darwin for example left a deadly legacy of sceptical atheistic thinking that has ensured that millions will go to their graves without discovering the beauty of a relationship with their Creator because they believed in the myth of evolution.

'A hundred years from now it will not matter what kind of house I lived in, how much money I had, nor what my clothes were like. But the world may be a little better because I was important in the life of a child.'

Dr. Forest E. Witcraft

Your legacy comprises both ends and means. Winning in and of itself is not enough. The means by which you move through your life will be a big part of how you are remembered. Integrity, patience, honesty and respect are all qualities that are a big part of an inspiring legacy. How can your accomplishments be admired for posterity when every time you think about how you achieved them, you want to blush in embarrassment?

'What good is it for a man to gain the whole world, and yet forfeit or lose his very self?' **(Luke 9:25)**

Think. Really think. The beauty of considering your legacy is the clarity it brings to daily decisions. Each decision moves you closer to or further from your legacy. Make this life of yours into a work of art.

William Borden was a very wealthy man. When God touched his life, he got rid of his fortune, and became a missionary. Whilst in the mission field, he contracted a disease and died soon afterwards. His final thoughts have become his legacy and should challenge us too: "No reserves. No retreats. No regrets." Most of us would conclude that his life was a waste. But William Borden's legacy in an untimely death has touched more people than he might have ever reached had he lived

We all have a life to live. What do you really wish to accomplish? What would you like to leave behind? All of our decisions are significant and the decisions we make today will influence our future and our families' futures also. What commitment, decisions and actions must you take today to ensure that you leave behind a good name and a godly heritage?

I know that you will choose well.

Printed in the United States
by Baker & Taylor Publisher Services